Robert Louis Stevenson was born in Edinburgh in 1850, and educated at Edinburgh Academy and Edinburgh University. Both his father and his grandfather had been lighthouse-builders, and Stevenson planned to emulate them: but the weakness of the lungs from which he suffered all his life made this inadvisable, and he switched from engineering to the law. His main interest lay in literature, however, and by the time he left university he was already contributing to various journals. His first book, *An Inland Voyage,* described a trip he made through France by canoe in 1876; a later journey, this time by land, formed the subject of *Travels with a Donkey in the Cevennes.* While on his travels he met and fell in love with Fanny Osbourne, an American woman ten years older than him and estranged from her husband. Once she had obtained her divorce, Stevenson sailed to America to join her in 1879 – the journey described in *The Amateur Emigrant* – and they were married in California. The following year he returned to Scotland: *Treasure Island* was published in 1882, and its success marked the turning point in Stevenson's career as a writer. Moving first to Switzerland and then to the Riviera in search of health, he wrote *The Black Arrow* and *A Child's Garden of Verses* before returning to England. He settled in Bournemouth in 1884, publishing *Kidnapped* in 1886. In 1887 he sailed again to America, settling finally in Samoa in 1890. He died of a brain haemorrhage in 1894 at the age of forty-four. His other books include *The Master of Ballantrae, Catriona* and *The Strange Case of Dr Jekyll and Mr Hyde.*

THE AMATEUR EMIGRANT

Published in 1984 by
The Hogarth Press
40 William IV Street, London WC2N 4DF

The Amateur Emigrant was first published in its complete form in the
Edinburgh Edition of Stevenson's works, Chatto & Windus *et al*, 1895;
Part II, *Across the Plains*, had originally been published in book form by
Chatto & Windus, 1892.
Hogarth edition offset from the Skerryvore Edition, Wm Heinemann *et al*, 1925
Introduction copyright © Jonathan Raban 1984

British Library
Cataloguing in Publication Data
Stevenson, Robert Louis
The amateur emigrant.
1. Great Britain-Emigration and immigration
2. United States-Emigration and immigration
I. Title
304.8'3'4107   JV7618.N7
ISBN 0-7012-1912-2

Printed in Great Britain by
Cox & Wyman Ltd
Reading, Berkshire

CONTENTS

Introduction

Part I: From The Clyde to Sandy Hook

Part II: Across The Plains

INTRODUCTION

Too much of Stevenson's work is marred for the modern reader by its desolate and ingratiating charm. As John Bayley has said, it tends to smack of 'what I did on my hols'. Scotland, the Rhine, the Cevennes, the South Seas all rise from Stevenson's writing at its worst like images from a travel agent's brochure; over-coloured, drained of reality. *The Amateur Emigrant* is a triumphant exception to this general rule. It is a black book – Stevenson's blackest by far. As a document it is, quite simply, the best account ever written of *the* great European adventure in the nineteenth century, the passage to America, the New World. It is, though, far more than a document. It has the resonance and simplicity of a myth. Its secret subject is the nature of personal identity – the same theme that Stevenson pursued, in a schematic and sensational way, in *Dr Jekyll and Mr Hyde*. For the first and, regrettably, the last time in his career, Stevenson found in the form of the workaday travel book a marvellously subtle and elastic vehicle for his imaginative concerns. *The Amateur Emigrant* is a living nightmare, and a masterpiece.

The extraordinary quality of the book can be partly – and only partly – explained by the extraordinariness, for Stevenson himself, of the journey it describes. When he sailed from the Clyde for New York in 1879, Stevenson was not on his hols; he was travelling in deadly earnest. The decision to go to America was the most important one in his life.

He was twenty-eight. He had already idled wistfully with his donkey in the hills, and in a canoe on the Rhine waterway system, in *Travels with a Donkey* and *An Inland Voyage*. He was making a bare living as an essayist and reviewer. His lungs were in bad shape and he was chronically feverish; it was no accident that his writing up till now had mostly reported the peregrinations of an invalid in search of sun and fresh air.

Three years before, he had met Fanny Osbourne at Fontainebleau. Mrs Osbourne was an American, separated from her husband, with two children in tow. She and Stevenson fell in love; then she returned to San Francisco. In 1879, she telegraphed Stevenson in Edinburgh, begging him to join her. His father, appalled at the prospect of this scandalous match, refused to contribute a penny to Stevenson's transatlantic fare. After a violent row with his parents, the sickly young writer took ship. He was breaking with Europe, with his family, with his entire past. Despite the title of his book, there was nothing amateurish about his emigration.

He was poor, but it was love, and not poverty, that drove him to cross the Atlantic. Fanny Osbourne's telegram caused him to take part in the most important mass odyssey of modern history, as he joined the poor of Europe in their search for new life in a promised land. Embarking at Clydebank in the company of the unemployed of Scotland and Northern England, he was at one with the Jewish peasants sailing from Bremerhaven, Swedes from Gothenberg, Italians from Naples, Irish from Cork. Most travelled 'steerage class' (named because the accommodations were originally around the rudder of the ship), in unventilated holds below the waterline. Disease spread easily in these beastly conditions, and many people died on the way.

The ordeal of the voyage (which lasted anything from ten days to four weeks) separated the two worlds of Europe and America in much the same way as Purgatory separates Hell and Heaven – at least, that is how it has been seen in literature. The miseries of travelling in steerage became a powerful symbol of the rift between the two continents, their cultures and histories, and of the profound sea-change wrought on the individual in his passage to becoming an American. Again and again in American fiction – especially in novels written by American Jews, from Abraham Cahan's *The Rise of David Levinsky* to Henry Roth's *Call It Sleep* – the Atlantic crossing was given the heightened meaning of a legendary event, a new chapter in the Book of Exodus.

No one, though, brought the authority of first-hand experience to these descriptions. Established writers did not travel in steerage; and the novelists were nearly all American-born, reliant on parents and grandparents for stories of how it was. Stevenson's position was unique: he went as a poor man; unlike the Jews of Eastern Europe, he was an English-speaker; and he was a professional writer with a notebook. The pressure of his own circumstances saved him from being a mere reporter or a tourist. As a result, *The Amateur Emigrant,* with its classic American subject, has a richness of detail and feeling that is unmatched in American literature.

It's clear that Stevenson did not mean to write a very ambitious book. He would have been happy, I think, if he had been able to cast his experience in the whimsical, digressive form that had brought him a good deal of success in *Travels with a Donkey*. The 'Amateur' of the title has a bright, belle-lettristic ring to it; so do chapter-titles like 'Steerage Scenes' and 'Steerage Types'. Early on, he tries to ramble gaily in his old manner, and there are a few passages of routinely 'lyrical' natural description.

Yet something is obviously wrong. The formula won't fit. Whatever happened to Stevenson on the exhausting journey by boat and train to San Francisco, it was too momentous, perhaps too terrible, to write out in his usual style of limp dandification. Instead, the experience itself seems to have taken hold of Stevenson and dictated its own form, powerfully overriding the author's original intentions.

The form eventually taken by *The Amateur Emigrant* is that of a *rite de passage*; it has the ritual structure of a marriage service or a funeral. The old self undergoes a symbolic death; the soul is put to trial and shriven; a new self is born in glory at the end of the rite. It is an immensely strong and evocative pattern; everywhere in the book, Stevenson seems to be governed by it more by instinct than by any conscious will to shape his writing to its demands.

From the beginning, it is made subtly evident that the

emigrant steamer and its human cargo have a significance that goes well beyond the literal and the journalistic. The ship is a close cousin to Brant's fifteenth-century *Narrenschiff*, the ship of fools. 'We were a company of the rejected; the drunken, the incompetent, the weak, the prodigal, all who had been unable to prevail against circumstances in the one land, were now fleeing pitifully to another; and though one or two might still succeed, all had already failed. We were a shipful of failures, the broken men of England.' The tone here is important. It is one of many passages where Stevenson is explicitly writing in the ceremonial language of the prayer book. Something solemn, important and universal is going on here; something way over the top of the conventional accuracies and details of realism.

Almost immediately, the old self of the emigrant starts to dissolve. First, he loses his class. In Europe he was a 'gentle-man'; on board ship, the only reminder of that lost status is a brass plate on the door of a lavatory – 'I was like one with a patent of nobility in a drawer at home; and when I felt out of spirits I could go down and refresh myself with a look of that brass plate.' Next, he loses his occupation. To the amusement of his fellow-passengers, he spends most of each day writing. Eventually, nailed as 'a writer', he is given the passenger list and told to reproduce it in copybook. Finally, on the train, he loses his name. He refuses to tell it to a curious stranger, and takes the nickname 'Shakespeare'.

These are not, of course, just ritual losses. They are part of the humiliating experience of every emigrant. In bare outline, they define what it means to be uprooted from one's country and one's past. In *The Amateur Emigrant*, though, one watches Stevenson conducting a curiously Jekyll-like experiment. He is fascinated by the process of becoming a nobody. 'I was travelling . . . out of myself.' Nameless, jobless, shorn of his personal history, his identity is perfectly fluid. At one moment, he is taken to be a seaman; at another, a musician. The rigours of the trip turn Stevenson into a lost soul, charging across America in the company of millions of other souls, all equally lost.

This appalled, phantasmagoric vision makes Stevenson's account of the United States read much like a report on Inferno. He has no time at all for the usual nineteenth-century pieties about the Melting Pot, Westward Expansion, or the notion of America as Liberty, welcoming the poor of Europe with compassionate open arms. What he sees are restless souls in torment:

It was still westward that they ran. Hunger, you would have thought, came out of the east like the sun, and the evening was made of edible gold. And, meantime, in the car in front of me, were there not half a hundred emigrants from the opposite quarter? Hungry Europe and hungry China, each pouring from their gates in search of provender, had here come face to face. The two waves had met; east and west had alike failed; the whole round world had been prospected and condemned; there was no El Dorado anywhere; and till one could emigrate to the moon, it seemed as well to stay patiently at home. Nor was there wanting another sign, at once more picturesque and more disheartening; for, as we continued to steam westward towards the land of gold, we were continually passing other emigrant trains upon the journey east; and these were as crowded as our own. Had all these return voyagers made a fortune in the mines? Were they all bound for Paris, and to be in Rome by Easter? It would seem not, for, whenever we met them, the passengers ran on to the platform and cried to us through the windows, in a kind of wailing chorus, to 'come back'. On the plains of Nebraska, in the mountains of Wyoming, it was still the same cry, and dismal to my heart, 'Come back!'

This is the nadir of the journey, Stevenson's darkest night of the soul. In the enormous emptinesses of Nebraska and Wyoming (where the settler's eye 'must embrace at every glance the whole seeming concave of the visible world; it quails before so vast an outlook, it is tortured by distance . . .'), the sick emigrant, crouched in a corner of the railroad car, is shriven.

In the final chapter the *rite de passage* is completed; the emigrant reborn in the green landscape of northern California. Greeting the river, the pine forest and the coloured sky, Stevenson writes 'It was like meeting one's wife'. Indeed, a real wedding was in the offing; Fanny Osbourne, now divorced, married Stevenson in 1880. The marriage in the book, though, is an exact and brilliant symbol. The old European is dead, the emigrant purged. He comes to California as a bridegroom.

The symbolic structure of *The Amateur Emigrant* is vital to the book. It is its hidden engine, giving it the pace and depth of a fine novel. Yet the real marvel of the thing is the way that Stevenson keeps the book continuously working at two separate levels. On one level there is the story, Dostoevskian in tone and execution, of the dissolution of an identity in a landscape close to that of Hell. On another, there is a heartbreakingly vivid documentary account of a real sea voyage, a real train journey.

For Stevenson's temperament was instinctively sceptical and empirical. He hoarded detail for its own sake. He was an immensely careful and sympathetic observer of other people's lives. When he came to deal with the physical conditions of the ship and the train, and with the characters of the emigrants, he was a scrupulous miniaturist. Every page of *The Amateur Emigrant* is dotted about with the trifles of life – with smells, fragments of dialect speech, clothes, facial expressions. It has the dense and varied texture of a true record.

Stevenson never wrote anything like this again. His next essay in travel, *The Silverado Squatters*, goes straight back to the cheerful whimsy of *Travels with a Donkey*. His fiction is obsessed with the dangerous identity games that he first explored in *The Amateur Emigrant*, but there they are distanced, seen through the reducing glass of gothic mannerism.

The book looks now like a lucky accident of history. In 1879, Stevenson happened to be going to the right place at the right time. Chance threw him the subject of his life; the story that he made of it is, I think, the best book he ever wrote – a marvellous piece of writing, lakelike in its lucidity and depth, part fact, part fiction, a genuine original.

Jonathan Raban, London 1983

DEDICATION

TO

ROBERT ALAN MOWBRAY STEVENSON

Our friendship was not only founded before we were born by a community of blood, but is in itself near as old as my life. It began with our early ages, and, like a history, has been continued to the present time. Although we may not be old in the world, we are old to each other, having so long been intimates. We are now widely separated, a great sea and continent intervening; but memory, like care, mounts into iron ships and rides post behind the horseman. Neither time nor space nor enmity can conquer old affection; and as I dedicate these sketches, it is not to you only, but to all in the old country, that I send the greeting of my heart.

ROBERT LOUIS STEVENSON.

1879.

THE
AMATEUR
EMIGRANT

PART I
FROM THE CLYDE
TO SANDY HOOK

THE SECOND CABIN

I FIRST encountered my fellow-passengers on the Broomielaw in Glasgow. Thence we descended the Clyde in no familiar spirit, but looking askance on each other as on possible enemies. A few Scandinavians, who had already grown acquainted on the North Sea, were friendly and voluble over their long pipes; but among English speakers distance and suspicion reigned supreme. The sun was soon overclouded, the wind freshened and grew sharp as we continued to descend the widening estuary; and with the falling temperature the gloom among the passengers increased. Two of the women wept. Anyone who had come aboard might have supposed we were all absconding from the law. There was scarce a word interchanged, and no common sentiment but that of cold united us, until at length, having touched at Greenock, a pointing arm and a rush to the starboard now announced that our ocean steamer was in sight. There she lay in mid-river, at the tail of the Bank, her sea-signal flying: a wall of bulwark, a street of white deck-houses, an inspiring forest of spars, larger than a church, and soon to be as populous as many an incorporated town in the land to which she was to bear us.

I was not, in truth, a steerage passenger. Although anxious to see the worst of emigrant life, I had some work to finish on the voyage, and was advised to go by the second cabin, where at least I should have a table at command. The advice was excellent; but to understand the choice, and what I gained, some outline of the internal disposition of the ship will first be neces-

5

sary. In her very nose is Steerage No. 1, down two pair of stairs. A little abaft, another companion, labelled Steerage No. 2 and 3, gives admission to three galleries, two running forward towards Steerage No. 1, and the third aft towards the engines. The starboard forward gallery is the second cabin. Away abaft the engines and below the officers' cabins, to complete our survey of the vessel, there is yet a third nest of steerages, labelled 4 and 5. The second cabin, to return, is thus a modified oasis in the very heart of the steerages. Through the thin partition you can hear the steerage passengers being sick, the rattle of tin dishes as they sit at meals, the varied accents in which they converse, the crying of their children terrified by this new experience, or the clean flat smack of the parental hand in chastisement.

There are, however, many advantages for the inhabitant of this strip. He does not require to bring his own bedding or dishes, but finds berths and a table completely if somewhat roughly furnished. He enjoys a distinct superiority in diet; but this, strange to say, differs not only on different ships, but on the same ship according as her head is to the east or west. In my own experience, the principal difference between our table and that of the true steerage passenger was the table itself, and the crockery plates from which we ate. But lest I should show myself ungrateful, let me recapitulate every advantage. At breakfast, we had a choice between tea and coffee for beverage; a choice not easy to make, the two were so surprisingly alike. I found that I could sleep after the coffee and lay awake after the tea, which is proof conclusive of some chemical disparity; and even by the palate I could distinguish a smack of snuff in the former from a flavour of boiling and dish-cloths in the second. As a matter of fact, I have seen passengers, after many sips, still doubting which had been supplied them. In the way of eatables at the same meal we were gloriously favoured; for in addition to porridge, which was common to all, we had Irish stew, sometimes a bit of fish, and sometimes rissoles. The dinner of soup, roast fresh beef, boiled salt junk, and potatoes, was, I believe, exactly common to the steerage and the second cabin; only I have heard it rumoured that our potatoes were of a superior brand; and twice a week, on pudding-days, instead of duff, we had a saddlebag filled with currants under the name of a plum-pudding. At tea we were served with some broken meat from the saloon; sometimes in the comparatively elegant form of spare patties or rissoles; but as a general thing, mere chicken-bones and flakes of fish, neither hot nor cold. If these were not the scrapings of plates their looks belied them sorely; yet we were all too hungry to be proud, and fell to these leavings greedily. These, the bread, which was excellent, and the soup and porridge, which were both good, formed my whole diet throughout the voyage; so that except for the broken meat and the convenience of a table I might as well have been in the steerage outright. Had they given me porridge again in the evening I should have been perfectly contented with the fare. As it was, with a few biscuits and some whisky and water before turning in, I kept my body going and my spirits up to the mark.

The last particular in which the second-cabin passenger remarkably stands ahead of his brother of the steerage is one altogether of sentiment. In the steerage there are males and females; in the second cabin ladies and gentlemen. For some time after I came aboard I thought I was only a male; but in the course of a voyage of discovery between decks, I came on a brass plate, and learned that I was still a gentleman. Nobody knew it, of course. I was lost in the crowd of males and females, and rigorously confined to the same quarter of the deck. Who could tell whether I housed on the port or starboard side of Steerage No. 2 and 3? And it was only there that my superiority became practical; everywhere else I was incognito, moving among my inferiors with simplicity, not so much as a swagger to indicate that I was a gentleman after all, and had broken meat to tea. Still, I was like one with a patent of nobility in a drawer at home; and when I felt out of spirits I could go down and refresh myself with a look of that brass plate.

For all these advantages I paid but two guineas. Six guineas is the steerage fare; eight that by the second cabin; and when you remember that the steerage passenger must supply bedding and dishes, and, in five cases out of ten, either brings some dainties with him, or privately pays the steward for extra rations, the difference in price becomes almost nominal. Air comparatively fit to breathe, food comparatively varied, and the satisfaction of being still privately a gentleman, may thus be had almost for the asking. Two of my fellow-passengers in the second cabin had already made the passage by the cheaper fare, and declared it was an experiment not to be repeated. As I go on to tell about my steerage friends, the reader will perceive that they were not alone in their opinion. Out of ten with whom I was more or less intimate, I am sure not fewer than five vowed, if they returned, to travel second cabin; and all who had left their wives behind them assured me they would go without the comfort of their presence until they could afford to bring them by saloon.

Our party in the second cabin was not perhaps the most interesting on board. Perhaps even in the saloon there was as much goodwill and character. Yet it had some elements of curiosity. There was a mixed group of Swedes, Danes, and Norsemen, one of whom, gener-

ally known by the name of " Johnny," in spite of his
own protests, greatly diverted us by his clever cross-
country efforts to speak English, and became on the
strength of that an universal favourite—it takes so
little in this world of shipboard to create a popularity.
There was, besides, a Scots mason, known from his
favourite dish as " Irish Stew," three or four non-
descript Scots, a fine young Irishman, O'Reilly, and
a pair of young men who deserve a special word of
condemnation. One of them was Scots; the other
claimed to be American; admitted, after some fencing,
that he was born in England; and ultimately proved
to be an Irishman born and nurtured, but ashamed to
own his country. He had a sister on board, whom he
faithfully neglected throughout the voyage, though she
was not only sick, but much his senior, and had nursed
and cared for him in childhood. In appearance he was
like an imbecile Henry the Third of France. The
Scotsman, though perhaps as big an ass, was not so
dead of heart; and I have only bracketed them together
because they were fast friends, and disgraced themselves equally by their conduct at the table.

Next, to turn to topics more agreeable, we had a
newly married couple, devoted to each other, with a
pleasant story of how they had first seen each other
years ago at a preparatory school, and that very afternoon he had carried her books home for her. I do not
know if this story will be plain to Southern readers;
but to me it recalls many a school idyll, with wrathful
swains of eight and nine confronting each other stride-
legs, flushed with jealousy; for to carry home a young
lady's books was both a delicate attention and a
privilege.

Then there was an old lady, or indeed I am not sure
that she was as much old as antiquated and strangely
out of place, who had left her husband, and was travel-

ling all the way to Kansas by herself. We had to take
her own word that she was married; for it was sorely
contradicted by the testimony of her appearance.
Nature seemed to have sanctified her for the single
state; even the colour of her hair was incompatible with
matrimony, and her husband, I thought, should be a
man of saintly spirit and phantasmal bodily presence.
She was ill, poor thing; her soul turned from the
viands; the dirty tablecloth shocked her like an impro-
priety; and the whole strength of her endeavour was
bent upon keeping her watch true to Glasgow time till
she should reach New York. They had heard reports,
her husband and she, of some unwarrantable disparity
of hours between these two cities; and with a spirit
commendably scientific, had seized on this occasion to
put them to the proof. It was a good thing for the old
lady; for she passed much leisure time in studying the
watch. Once, when prostrated by sickness, she let it
run down. It was inscribed on her harmless mind in
letters of adamant that the hands of a watch must never
be turned backwards; and so it behoved her to lie in
wait for the exact moment ere she started it again.
When she imagined this was about due, she sought
out one of the young second-cabin Scotsmen, who was
embarked on the same experiment as herself and had
hitherto been less neglectful. She was in quest of two
o'clock; and when she learned it was already seven on
the shores of Clyde, she lifted up her voice and cried
"Gravy!" I had not heard this innocent expletive
since I was a young child; and I suppose it must have
been the same with the other Scotsmen present, for we
all laughed our fill.

Last but not least, I come to my excellent friend Mr.
Jones. It would be difficult to say whether I was his
right-hand man, or he mine, during the voyage. Thus
at table I carved, while he only scooped gravy; but at

our concerts, of which more anon, he was the president
who called up performers to sing, and I but his mes-
senger who ran his errands and pleaded privately with
the over-modest. I knew I liked Mr. Jones from the
moment I saw him. I thought him by his face to be
Scottish; nor could his accent undeceive me. For as
there is a *lingua franca* of many tongues on the moles
and in the feluccas of the Mediterranean, so there is
a free or common accent among English-speaking men
who follow the sea. They catch a twang in a New
England port; from a Cockney skipper, even a Scotsman sometimes learns to drop an *h*; a word of a dialect
is picked up from another hand in the forecastle; until
often the result is undecipherable, and you have to ask
for the man's place of birth. So it was with Mr. Jones.
I thought him a Scotsman who had been long to sea;
and yet he was from Wales, and had been most of his
life a blacksmith at an inland forge; a few years in
America and half a score of ocean voyages having
sufficed to modify his speech into the common pattern.
By his own account he was both strong and skilful in
his trade. A few years back, he had been married, and
after a fashion a rich man; now the wife was dead and
the money gone. But his was the nature that looks
forward, and goes on from one year to another and
through all the extremities of fortune undismayed;
and if the sky were to fall to-morrow, I should look to
see Jones, the day following, perched on a step-ladder
and getting things to rights. He was always hovering
round inventions like a bee over a flower, and lived in
a dream of patents. He had with him a patent medicine,
for instance, the composition of which he had bought
years ago for five dollars from an American pedlar, and
sold the other day for a hundred pounds (I think it
was) to an English apothecary. It was called Golden
Oil; cured all maladies without exception; and I am

EARLY IMPRESSIONS

We steamed out of the Clyde on Thursday night, and early on the Friday afternoon we took in our last batch of emigrants at Lough Foyle, in Ireland, and said farewell to Europe. The company was now complete, and began to draw together, by inscrutable magnetisms, upon the decks. There were Scots and Irish in plenty, a few English, a few Americans, a good handful of Scandinavians, a German or two, and one Russian; all now belonging for ten days to one small iron country on the deep.

As I walked the deck and looked round upon my fellow-passengers, thus curiously assorted from all northern Europe, I began for the first time to understand the nature of emigration. Day by day throughout the passage, and thenceforward across all the States, and on to the shores of the Pacific, this knowledge grew more clear and melancholy. Emigration, from a word of the most cheerful import, came to sound most dismally in my ear. There is nothing more agreeable to picture and nothing more pathetic to behold. The abstract idea, as conceived at home, is hopeful and adventurous. A young man, you fancy, scorning restraints and helpers, issues forth into life, that great battle, to fight for his own hand. The most pleasant stories of ambition, of difficulties overcome, and of ultimate success, are but as episodes to this great epic of self-help. The epic is composed of individual heroisms; it stands to them as the victorious war which subdued an empire stands to the personal act of bravery which spiked a single cannon and was adequately rewarded with a medal. For in emigration the young men enter direct and by the shipload on their heritage of work; empty continents swarm, as at the bo's'un's whistle, with industrious hands, and whole new empires are domesticated to the service of man.

This is the closet picture, and is found, on trial, to consist mostly of embellishments. The more I saw of my fellow-passengers, the less I was tempted to the lyric note. Comparatively few of the men were below thirty; many were married, and encumbered with families; not a few were already up in years; and this itself was out of tune with my imaginations, for the ideal emigrant should certainly be young. Again, I thought he should offer to the eye some bold type of humanity, with bluff or hawk-like features, and the stamp of an eager and pushing disposition. Now those around me were for the most part quiet, orderly, obedient citizens, family men broken by adversity, elderly youths who had failed to place themselves in life, and people who had seen better days. Mildness was the prevailing character; mild mirth and mild endurance. In a word, I was not taking part in an impetuous and conquering sally, such as swept over Mexico or Siberia, but found myself, like Marmion, " in the lost battle, borne down by the flying."

Labouring mankind had in the last years, and throughout Great Britain, sustained a prolonged and crushing series of defeats. I had heard vaguely of these reverses; of whole streets of houses standing deserted by the Tyne, the cellar-doors broken and removed for firewood; of homeless men loitering at the street-corners of Glasgow with their chests beside them; of closed factories, useless strikes, and starving girls. But I had never taken them home to me or represented these distresses livingly to my imagination. A turn of the market may be a calamity as disastrous as the French retreat from Moscow; but it hardly lends itself to lively treatment, and makes a trifling figure in the morning papers. We may struggle as we please, we are not born economists. The individual is more affecting than the mass. It is by the scenic accidents, and the appeal to the carnal eye, that for the most part we grasp the significance of tragedies. Thus it was only now, when I found myself involved in the rout, that I began to appreciate how sharp had been the battle. We were a company of the rejected; the drunken, the incompetent, the weak, the prodigal, all who had been unable to prevail against circumstances in the one land, were now fleeing pitifully to another; and though one or two might still succeed, all had already failed. We were a shipful of failures, the broken men of England. Yet it must not be supposed that these people exhibited depression. The scene, on the contrary, was cheerful. Not a tear was shed on board the vessel. All were full of hope for the future, and showed an inclination to innocent gaiety. Some were heard to sing, and all began to scrape acquaintance with small jests and ready laughter.

The children found each other out like dogs, and ran about the decks scraping acquaintance after their fashion also. " What do you call your mither? " I heard one ask. " Mawmaw," was the reply, indicating, I fancy, a shade of difference in the social scale. When people pass each other on the high seas of life at so early an age the contact is but slight, and the relation more like what we may imagine to be the friendship of flies than that of men; it is so quickly joined, so easily dissolved, so open in its communications and so devoid of deeper human qualities. The children, I observed, were all in a band, and as thick as thieves at a fair, while their elders were still ceremoniously manœuvring on the outskirts of acquaintance. The sea, the ship, and the seamen were soon as familiar as home to these half-conscious little ones. It was odd to hear them, throughout the voyage, employ shore words to designate portions of the vessel. " Co' 'way doon to yon dyke," I heard one say, probably meaning the bulwark. I often had my heart in my mouth, watching them climb into the shrouds or on the rails, while the ship went swinging through the waves; and I admired and envied the courage of their mothers, who sat by in the sun and looked on with composure at these perilous feats. " He'll maybe be a sailor," I heard one remark; " now's the time to learn." I had been on the point of running forward to interfere, but stood back at that, reproved. Very few in the more delicate classes have the nerve to look upon the peril of one dear to them; but the life of poorer folk, where necessity is so much more immediate and imperious, braces even a mother to this extreme of endurance. And perhaps, after all, it is better that the lad should break his neck than that you should break his spirit.

And since I am here on the chapter of the children, I must mention one little fellow, whose family belonged to Steerage No. 4 and 5, and who, wherever he went, was like a strain of music round the ship. He was an ugly, merry, unbreeched child of three, his lint-white hair in a tangle, his face smeared with suet and treacle; but he ran to and fro with so natural a step, and fell and picked himself up again with such grace and good-humour, that he might fairly be called beautiful when he was in motion. To meet him, crowing with laughter and beating an accompaniment to his own mirth with a tin spoon upon a tin cup, was to meet a little triumph of the human species. Even when his mother and the rest of his family lay sick and prostrate around him, he sat upright in their midst and sang aloud in the pleasant heartlessness of infancy.

Throughout the Friday, intimacy among us men made but a few advances. We discussed the probable duration of the voyage, we exchanged pieces of information, naming our trades, what we hoped to find in the new world, or what we were fleeing from in the old; and, above all, we condoled together over the food and the vileness of the steerage. One or two had been so near famine that you may say they had run into the ship with the devil at their heels; and to these all seemed for the best in the best of possible steamers. But the majority were hugely discontented. Coming as they did from a country in so low a state as Great Britain, many of them from Glasgow, which commercially speaking was as good as dead, and many having long been out of work, I was surprised to find them so dainty in their notions. I myself lived almost exclusively on bread, porridge, and soup, precisely as it was supplied to them, and found it, if not luxurious, at least sufficient. But these working men were loud in their outcries. It was not " food for human beings," it was " only fit for pigs," it was " a disgrace." Many of them lived almost entirely upon biscuit, others on their own private supplies, and some paid extra for better rations from the ship. This marvellously changed my notion of the degree of luxury habitual to the artisan. I was prepared to hear him grumble, for grumbling is the traveller's pastime; but I was not prepared to find him turn away from a diet which was palatable to myself. Words I should have disregarded, or taken with a liberal allowance; but when a man prefers dry biscuit there can be no question of the sincerity of his disgust.

With one of their complaints I could most heartily sympathise. A single night of the steerage had filled them with horror. I had myself suffered, even in my decent second-cabin berth, from the lack of air; and as the night promised to be fine and quiet, I determined to sleep on deck, and advised all who complained of their quarters to follow my example. I daresay a dozen of others agreed to do so, and I thought we should have been quite a party. Yet, when I brought up my rug about seven bells, there was no one to be seen but the watch. That chimerical terror of good night-air, which makes men close their windows, list their doors, and seal themselves up with their own poisonous exhalations, had sent all these healthy workmen down below. One would think we had been brought up in a fever country; yet in England the most malarious districts are in the bed-chambers.

I felt saddened at this defection, and yet half-pleased to have the night so quietly to myself. The wind had hauled a little ahead on the starboard bow, and was dry but chilly. I found a shelter near the fire-hole, and made myself snug for the night. The ship moved over the uneven sea with a gentle and cradling movement. The ponderous, organic labours of the engine in her bowels occupied the mind, and prepared it for slumber. From time to time a heavier lurch would disturb me as I lay, and recall me to the obscure borders of consciousness; or I heard, as it were through a veil, the clear note of the clapper on the brass and the beautiful sea-cry, "All's well!" I know nothing, whether for poetry or music, that can surpass the effect of these two syllables in the darkness of a night at sea.

The day dawned fairly enough, and during the early part we had some pleasant hours to improve acquaintance in the open air; but towards nightfall the wind freshened, the rain began to fall, and the sea rose so high that it was difficult to keep one's footing on the deck. I have spoken of our concerts. We were indeed a musical ship's company, and cheered our way into exile with the fiddle, the accordion, and the songs of all nations. Good, bad, or indifferent—Scottish, English, Irish, Russian, German, or Norse—the songs were received with generous applause. Once or twice, a recitation, very spiritedly rendered in a powerful Scottish accent, varied the proceedings; and once we sought in vain to dance a quadrille, eight men of us together, to the music of the violin. The performers were all humorous, frisky fellows, who loved to cut capers in private life; but as soon as they were arranged for the dance, they conducted themselves like so many mutes at a funeral. I have never seen decorum pushed so far; and as this was not expected, the quadrille was soon whistled down, and the dancers departed under a cloud. Eight Frenchmen, even eight Englishmen from another rank of society, would have dared to make some fun for themselves and the spectators; but the working man, when sober, takes an extreme and even melancholy view of personal deportment. A fifth-form schoolboy is not more careful of dignity. He dares not be comical; his fun must escape from him unprepared, and, above all, it must be unaccompanied by any physical demonstration. I like his society under most circumstances, but let me never again join with him in public gambols.

But the impulse to sing was strong, and triumphed over modesty and even the inclemencies of sea and sky. On this rough Saturday night, we got together by the main deck-house, in a place sheltered from the wind and rain. Some clinging to a ladder which led to the hurricane deck, and the rest knitting arms or taking hands, we made a ring to support the women in the violent lurching of the ship; and when we were thus disposed, sang to our heart's content. Some of the songs were appropriate to the scene; others strikingly the reverse. Bastard doggerel of the music-hall, such as, "Around her splendid form, I weaved the magic circle," sounded bald, bleak, and pitifully silly. " We don't want to fight, but, by Jingo, if we do," was in some measure saved by the vigour and unanimity with which the chorus was thrown forth into the night. I observed a Platt-Deutsch mason, entirely innocent of

English, adding heartily to the general effect. And perhaps the German mason is but a fair example of the sincerity with which the song was rendered; for nearly all with whom I conversed upon the subject were bitterly opposed to war, and attributed their own misfortunes, and frequently their own taste for whisky, to the campaigns in Zululand and Afghanistan.

Every now and again, however, some song that touched the pathos of our situation was given forth; and you could hear by the voices that took up the burden how the sentiment came home to each. " The Anchor's Weighed " was true for us. We were indeed " Rocked on the bosom of the stormy deep." How many of us could say with the singer, " I'm lonely to-night, love, without you," or " Go, some one, and tell them from me, to write me a letter from home! " And when was there a more appropriate moment for "Auld Lang Syne " than now, when the land, the friends, and the affections of that mingled but beloved time were fading and fleeing behind us in the vessel's wake? It pointed forward to the hour when these labours should be overpast, to the return voyage, and to many a meeting in the sanded inn, when those who had parted in the spring of youth should again drink a cup of kindness in their age. Had not Burns contemplated emigration, I scarce believe he would have found that note.

All Sunday the weather remained wild and cloudy; many were prostrated by sickness; only five sat down to tea in the second cabin, and two of these departed abruptly ere the meal was at an end. The Sabbath was observed strictly by the majority of the emigrants. I heard an old woman express her surprise that " the ship didna gae doon," as she saw some one pass her with a chess-board on the holy day. Some sang Scottish psalms. Many went to service, and in true Scottish fashion came back ill pleased with their divine. " I didna think he was an experienced preacher," said one girl to me.

It was a bleak, uncomfortable day; but at night, by six bells, although the wind had not yet moderated, the clouds were all wrecked and blown away behind the rim of the horizon, and the stars came out thickly overhead. I saw Venus burning as steadily and sweetly across this hurly-burly of the winds and waters as ever at home upon the summer woods. The engine pounded, the screw tossed out of the water with a roar, and shook the ship from end to end; the bows battled with loud reports against the billows: and as I stood in the lee-scuppers and looked up to where the funnel leaned out, over my head, vomiting smoke, and the black and monstrous topsails blotted, at each lurch, a different crop of stars, it seemed as if all this trouble were a thing of small account, and that just above the mast reigned peace unbroken and eternal.

Our companion (Steerage No. 2 and 3) was a favourite resort. Down one flight of stairs there was a comparatively large open space, the centre occupied by a hatchway, which made a convenient seat for about twenty persons, while barrels, coils of rope, and the carpenter's bench afforded perches for perhaps as many more. The canteen, or steerage bar, was on one side of the stair; on the other, a no less attractive spot, the cabin of the indefatigable interpreter. I have seen people packed into this space like herrings in a barrel, and many merry evenings prolonged there until five bells, when the lights were ruthlessly extinguished and all must go to roost.

It had been rumoured since Friday that there was a fiddler aboard, who lay sick and unmelodious in Steerage No. 1; and on the Monday forenoon, as I came down the companion, I was saluted by something in Strathspey time. A white-faced Orpheus was cheerily playing to an audience of white-faced women. It was as much as he could do to play, and some of his hearers were scarce able to sit; yet they had crawled from their bunks at the first experimental flourish, and found better than medicine in the music. Some of the heaviest heads began to nod in time, and a degree of animation looked from some of the palest eyes. Humanly speaking, it is a more important matter to play the fiddle, even badly, than to write huge works upon recondite subjects. What could Mr. Darwin have done for these sick women? But this fellow scraped away; and the world was positively a better place for all who heard him. We have yet to understand the economical value of these mere accomplishments. I told the fiddler he was a happy man, carrying happiness about with him in his fiddle-case, and he seemed alive to the fact.

" It is a privilege," I said. He thought a while upon

the word, turning it over in his Scots head, and then answered with conviction, " Yes, a privilege."

That night I was summoned by " Merrily danced the Quaker's wife " into the companion of Steerage No. 4 and 5. This was, properly speaking, but a strip across a deck-house, lit by a sickly lantern which swung to and fro with the motion of the ship. Through the open slide-door we had a glimpse of a grey night sea, with patches of phosphorescent foam flying, swift as birds, into the wake, and the horizon rising and falling as the vessel rolled to the wind. In the centre the companion ladder plunged down sheerly like an open pit. Below, on the first landing, and lighted by another lamp, lads and lasses danced, not more than three at a time for lack of space, in jigs and reels and hornpipes. Above, on either side, there was a recess railed with iron, perhaps two feet wide and four long, which stood for orchestra and seats of honour. In the one balcony five slatternly Irish lasses sat woven in a comely group. In the other was posted Orpheus, his body, which was convulsively in motion, forming an odd contrast to his somnolent, imperturbable Scots face. His brother, a dark man with a vehement, interested countenance, who made a god of the fiddler, sat by with open mouth, drinking in the general admiration and throwing out remarks to kindle it.

" That's a bonny hornpipe now," he would say, " it's a great favourite with performers; they dance the sand dance to it." And he expounded the sand dance. Then suddenly it would be a long " Hush! " with uplifted finger and glowing, supplicating eyes; " he's going to play 'Auld Robin Gray' on one string! " And throughout this excruciating movement,—" On one string, that's on one string! " he kept crying. I would have given something myself that it had been on none; but the hearers were much awed. I called for a tune or two, and thus introduced myself to the notice of the brother, who directed his talk to me for some little while, keeping, I need hardly mention, true to his topic, like the seamen to the star. " He's grand of it," he said confidentially. " His master was a music-hall man." Indeed the music-hall man had left his mark, for our fiddler was ignorant of many of our best old airs; " Logie o' Buchan," for instance, he only knew as a quick, jigging figure in a set of quadrilles, and had never heard it called by name. Perhaps, after all, the brother was the more interesting performer of the two. I have spoken with him afterwards repeatedly, and found him always the same quick, fiery bit of a man, not without brains; but he never showed to such advantage as when he was thus squiring the fiddler into public note. There is nothing more becoming than a genuine admiration; and it shares this with love, that it does not become contemptible although misplaced.

The dancing was but feebly carried on. The space was almost impracticably small; and the Irish wenches combined the extreme of bashfulness about this innocent display with a surprising impudence and roughness of address. Most often, either the fiddle lifted up its voice unheeded, or only a couple of lads would be footing it and snapping fingers on the landing. And such was the eagerness of the brother to display all the acquirements of his idol, and such the sleepy indifference of the performer, that the tune would as often as not be changed, and the hornpipe expire into a ballad before the dancers had cut half a dozen shuffles.

In the meantime, however, the audience had been growing more and more numerous every moment; there was hardly standing-room round the top of the companion; and the strange instinct of the race moved some of the new-comers to close both the doors, so that the atmosphere grew insupportable. It was a good place, as the saying is, to leave.

The wind hauled ahead with a head sea. By ten at night heavy sprays were flying and drumming over the forecastle; the companion of Steerage No. 1 had to be closed, and the door of communication through the second cabin thrown open. Either from the convenience of the opportunity, or because we had already a number of acquaintances in that part of the ship, Mr. Jones and I paid it a late visit. Steerage No. 1 is shaped like an isosceles triangle, the sides opposite the equal angles bulging outward with the contour of the ship. It is lined with eight pens of sixteen bunks apiece, four bunks below and four above on either side. At night the place is lit with two lanterns, one to each table. As the steamer beat on her way among the rough billows, the light passed through violent phases of change, and was thrown to and fro and up and down with startling swiftness. You were tempted to wonder, as you looked, how so thin a glimmer could control and disperse such solid blackness. When Jones and I entered we found a little company of our acquaintances seated together at the triangular foremost table. A more forlorn party, in more dismal circumstances, it would be hard to imagine. The motion here in the ship's nose was very violent; the uproar of the sea often overpoweringly loud. The yellow flicker of the lantern spun round and round and tossed the shadows in masses. The air was hot, but it struck a chill from its fœtor. From all round in the dark bunks the scarcely human noises of the sick joined into a kind of farmyard chorus. In the midst, these five friends of mine were keeping up what heart they could in company. Singing was their refuge from discomfortable thoughts and sensations. One piped, in feeble tones, " O why left I my hame?" which seemed a pertinent question in the circumstances. Another, from the invisible horrors of a pen where he lay dog-sick upon the upper shelf, found courage, in a blink of his sufferings, to give us several verses of the "Death of Nelson"; and it was odd and eerie to hear the chorus breathe feebly from all sorts of dark corners, and "this day has done his dooty" rise and fall and be taken up again in this dim *inferno*, to an accompaniment of plunging, hollow-sounding bows and the rattling spray-showers overhead.

All seemed unfit for conversation; a certain dizziness had interrupted the activity of their minds; and except to sing they were tongue-tied. There was present, however, one tall, powerful fellow of doubtful nationality, being neither quite Scotsman nor altogether Irish, but of surprising clearness of conviction on the highest problems. He had gone nearly beside himself on the Sunday, because of a general backwardness to indorse his definition of mind as "a living, thinking substance which cannot be felt, heard, or seen"—nor, I presume, although he failed to mention it, smelt. Now he came forward in a pause with another contribution to our culture.

"Just by way of change," said he, "I'll ask you a Scripture riddle. There's profit in them too," he added ungrammatically.

This was the riddle—

> C and P
> Did agree
> To cut down C ;
> But C and P
> Could not agree
> Without the leave of G.
> All the people cried to see
> The crueltie
> Of C and P.

Harsh are the words of Mercury after the songs of
Apollo! We were a long while over the problem, shak-
ing our heads and gloomily wondering how a man
could be such a fool; but at length he put us out of
suspense and divulged the fact that C and P stood for
Caiaphas and Pontius Pilate.

I think it must have been the riddle that settled us;
but the motion and the close air likewise hurried our
departure. We had not been gone long, we heard next
morning, ere two or even three out of the five fell sick.
We thought it little wonder on the whole, for the sea
kept contrary all night. I now made my bed upon the
second cabin floor, where, although I ran the risk of
being stepped upon, I had a free current of air, more or
less vitiated indeed, and running only from steerage to
steerage, but at least not stagnant; and from this couch,
as well as the usual sounds of a rough night at sea, the
hateful coughing and retching of the sick and the sobs
of children, I heard a man run wild with terror beseech-
ing his friend for encouragement. " The ship's going
down! " he cried with a thrill of agony. " The ship's
going down! " he repeated, now in a blank whisper,
now with his voice rising towards a sob; and his friend
might reassure him, reason with him, joke at him—all
was in vain, and the old cry came back, " The ship's
going down! " There was something panicky and
catching in the emotion of his tones; and I saw in a
clear flash what an involved and hideous tragedy was a
disaster to an emigrant ship. If this whole parishful of
people came no more to land, into how many houses
would the newspaper carry woe, and what a great part
of the web of our corporate human life would be rent
across for ever!

The next morning when I came on deck I found a
new world indeed. The wind was fair; the sun mounted
into a cloudless heaven; through great dark blue seas

the ship cut a swath of curded foam. The horizon was dotted all day with companionable sails, and the sun shone pleasantly on the long, heaving deck.

We had many fine-weather diversions to beguile the time. There was a single chess-board and a single pack of cards. Sometimes as many as twenty of us would be playing dominoes for love. Feats of dexterity, puzzles for the intelligence, some arithmetical, some of the same order as the old problem of the fox and goose and cabbage, were always welcome; and the latter, I observed, more popular as well as more conspicuously well done than the former. We had a regular daily competition to guess the vessel's progress; and twelve o'clock, when the result was published in the wheel-house, came to be a moment of considerable interest. But the interest was unmixed. Not a bet was laid upon our guesses. From the Clyde to Sandy Hook I never heard a wager offered or taken. We had, besides, romps in plenty. Puss in the Corner, which we had re-baptised, in more manly style, Devil and four Corners, was my own favourite game; but there were many who preferred another, the humour of which was to box a person's ears until he found out who had cuffed him.

This Tuesday morning we were all delighted with the change of weather, and in the highest possible spirits. We got in a cluster like bees, sitting between each other's feet under lee of the deck-houses. Stories and laughter went around. The children climbed about the shrouds. White faces appeared for the first time, and began to take on colour from the wind. I was kept hard at work making cigarettes for one amateur after another, and my less than moderate skill was heartily admired. Lastly, down sat the fiddler in our midst and began to discourse his reels, and jigs, and ballads, with now and then a voice or two to take up the air and throw in the interest of human speech.

Through this merry and good-hearted scene there came three cabin passengers, a gentleman and two young ladies, picking their way with little gracious titters of indulgence, and a Lady-Bountiful air about nothing, which galled me to the quick. I have little of the radical in social questions, and have always nourished an idea that one person was as good as another. But I began to be troubled by this episode. It was astonishing what insults these people managed to convey by their presence. They seemed to throw their clothes in our faces. Their eyes searched us all over for tatters and incongruities. A laugh was ready at their lips; but they were too well-mannered to indulge it in our hearing. Wait a bit, till they were all back in the saloon, and then hear how wittily they would depict the manners of the steerage. We were in truth very innocently, cheerfully, and sensibly engaged, and there was no shadow of excuse for the swaying elegant superiority with which these damsels passed among us, or for the stiff and waggish glances of their squire. Not a word was said; only when they were gone Mackay sullenly damned their impudence under his breath; but we were all conscious of an icy influence and a dead break in the course of our enjoyment.

We had a fellow on board, an Irish-American, for all the world like a beggar in a print by Callot; one-eyed, with great, splay crow's-feet round the sockets; a knotty squab nose coming down over his moustache; a miraculous hat; a shirt that had been white, ay, ages long ago; an alpaca coat in its last sleeves; and, without hyperbole, no buttons to his trousers. Even in these rags and tatters, the man twinkled all over with impudence like a piece of sham jewellery; and I have heard him offer a situation to one of his fellow-passengers with the air of a lord. Nothing could overlie such a fellow; a kind of base success was written on his brow. He was then in his ill days; but I can imagine him in Congress with his mouth full of bombast and sawder. As we moved in the same circle, I was brought necessarily into his society. I do not think I ever heard him say anything that was true, kind, or interesting; but there was entertainment in the man's demeanour. You might call him a half-educated Irish Tigg.

Our Russian made a remarkable contrast to this impossible fellow. Rumours and legends were current in the steerages about his antecedents. Some said he was a Nihilist escaping; others set him down for a harmless spendthrift, who had squandered fifty thousand roubles, and whose father had now despatched him to America by way of penance. Either tale might flourish in security; there was no contradiction to be feared, for the hero spoke not one word of English. I got on with him lumberingly enough in broken German, and learnt from his own lips that he had been an apothecary. He carried the photograph of his betrothed in a pocket-book, and remarked that it did not do her justice. The cut of his head stood out from among the passengers with an air of startling strangeness. The first natural instinct was to take him for a desperado; but although the features, to our Western eyes, had a barbaric and unhomely cast, the eye both reassured and touched. It was large and very dark and soft, with an expression of dumb endurance, as if it had often looked on desperate circumstances and never looked on them without resolution.

He cried out when I used the word. " No, no," he said, " not resolution."

" The resolution to endure," I explained.

And then he shrugged his shoulders, and said, "*Ach, ja,*" with gusto, like a man who has been flattered in his favourite pretensions. Indeed, he was always hinting at some secret sorrow; and his life, he said, had been one of unusual trouble and anxiety; so the legends of the steerage may have represented at least some shadow of the truth. Once, and once only, he sang a song at our concerts; standing forth without embarrassment, his great stature somewhat humped, his long arms frequently extended, his Kalmuck head thrown backward. It was a suitable piece of music, as deep as a cow's bellow and wild like the White Sea. He was struck and charmed by the freedom and sociality of our manners. At home, he said, no one on a journey would speak to him, but those with whom he would not care to speak; thus unconsciously involving himself in the condemnation of his countrymen. But Russia was soon to be changed; the ice of the Neva was softening under the sun of civilisation; the new ideas, "*wie ein feines Violine,*" were audible among the big empty drum notes of Imperial diplomacy; and he looked to see a great revival, though with a somewhat indistinct and childish hope.

We had a father and son who made a pair of Jacks-of-all-trades. It was the son who sang the " Death of Nelson " under such contrarious circumstances. He was by trade a shearer of ship plates; but he could touch the organ, had led two choirs, and played the

31

flute and piccolo in a professional string band. His repertory of songs was, besides, inexhaustible, and ranged impartially from the very best to the very worst within his reach. Nor did he seem to make the least distinction between these extremes, but would cheerfully follow up " Tom Bowling " with "Around her splendid form."

The father, an old, cheery, small piece of manhood, could do everything connected with tinwork from one end of the process to the other, use almost every carpenter's tool, and make picture frames to boot. " I sat down with silver plate every Sunday," said he, " and pictures on the wall. I have made enough money to be rolling in my carriage. But, sir," looking at me unsteadily with his bright rheumy eyes, " I was troubled with a drunken wife." He took a hostile view of matrimony in consequence. " It's an old saying," he remarked: " God made 'em, and the devil he mixed 'em."

I think he was justified by his experience. It was a dreary story. He would bring home three pounds on Saturday, and on Monday all the clothes would be in pawn. Sick of the useless struggle, he gave up a paying contract, and contented himself with small and ill-paid jobs. "A bad job was as good as a good job for me," he said; " it all went the same way." Once the wife showed signs of amendment; she kept steady for weeks on end; it was again worth while to labour and to do one's best. The husband found a good situation some distance from home, and, to make a little upon every hand, started the wife in a cook-shop; the children were here and there, busy as mice; savings began to grow together in the bank, and the golden age of hope had returned again to that unhappy family. But one week my old acquaintance, getting earlier through with his work, came home on the Friday instead of the Saturday, and there was his wife to receive him reeling drunk. He " took and gave her a pair o' black eyes," for which I pardon him, nailed up the cook-shop door, gave up his situation, and resigned himself to a life of poverty, with the workhouse at the end. As the children came to their full age they fled the house, and established themselves in other countries; some did well, some not so well; but the father remained at home alone with his drunken wife, all his sound-hearted pluck and varied accomplishments depressed and negatived.

Was she dead now? or, after all these years, had he broken the chain, and run from home like a schoolboy? I could not discover which; but here at least he was out on the adventure, and still one of the bravest and most youthful men on board.

" Now, I suppose, I must put my old bones to work again," said he; " but I can do a turn yet."

And the son to whom he was going, I asked, was he not able to support him?

"Oh yes," he replied. " But I'm never happy without a job on hand. And I'm stout; I can eat a'most anything. You see no craze about me."

This tale of a drunken wife was paralleled on board by another of a drunken father. He was a capable man, with a good chance in life; but he had drunk up two thriving businesses like a bottle of sherry, and involved his sons along with him in ruin. Now they were on board with us, fleeing his disastrous neighbourhood.

Total abstinence, like all ascetical conclusions, is unfriendly to the most generous, cheerful, and human parts of man; but it could have adduced many instances and arguments from among our ship's company. I was one day conversing with a kind and happy Scotsman, running to fat and perspiration in the physical, but with a taste for poetry and a genial sense of fun. I had asked him his hopes in emigrating. They were like those of

33

so many others, vague and unfounded; times were bad at home; they were said to have a turn for the better in the States; and a man could get on anywhere, he thought. That was precisely the weak point of his position; for if he could get on in America, why could he not do the same in Scotland? But I never had the courage to use that argument, though it was often on the tip of my tongue, and instead I agreed with him heartily, adding, with reckless originality, " if the man stuck to his work, and kept away from drink."

"Ah!" said he slowly, " the drink! You see, that's just my trouble."

He spoke with a simplicity that was touching, looking at me at the same time with something strange and timid in his eye, half-ashamed, half-sorry, like a good child who knows he should be beaten. You would have said he recognised a destiny to which he was born, and accepted the consequences mildly. Like the merchant Abudah, he was at the same time fleeing from his destiny and carrying it along with him, the whole at an expense of six guineas.

As far as I saw, drink, idleness, and incompetency were the three great causes of emigration, and for all of them, and drink first and foremost, this trick of getting transported overseas appears to me the silliest means of cure. You cannot run away from a weakness; you must some time fight it out or perish; and if that be so, why not now, and where you stand? *Cælum non animam.* Change Glenlivet for Bourbon, and it is still whisky, only not so good. A sea voyage will not give a man the nerve to put aside cheap pleasure; emigration has to be done before we climb the vessel; an aim in life is the only fortune worth the finding; and it is not to be found in foreign lands, but in the heart itself.

Speaking generally, there is no vice of this kind more contemptible than another; for each is but a result and

outward sign of a soul tragically shipwrecked. In the
majority of cases, cheap pleasure is resorted to by way
of anodyne. The pleasure-seeker sets forth upon life
with high and difficult ambitions; he meant to be nobly
good and nobly happy, though at as little pains as possible to himself; and it is because all has failed in his
celestial enterprise that you now behold him rolling in
the garbage. Hence the comparative success of the
teetotal pledge; because to a man who had nothing it
sets at least a negative aim in life. Somewhat as
prisoners beguile their days by taming a spider, the
reformed drunkard makes an interest out of abstaining
from intoxicating drinks, and may live for that nega-
tion. There is something, at least, *not to be done* each
day; and a cold triumph awaits him every evening.

We had one on board with us, whom I have already
referred to under the name of Mackay, who seemed to
me not only a good instance of this failure in life of
which we have been speaking, but a good type of the
intelligence which here surrounded me. Physically he
was a small Scotsman, standing a little back as though
he were already carrying the elements of a corporation,
and his looks somewhat marred by the smallness of his
eyes. Mentally, he was endowed above the average.
There were but few subjects on which he could not
converse with understanding and a dash of wit; de-
livering himself slowly and with gusto, like a man who
enjoyed his own sententiousness. He was a dry, quick,
pertinent debater, speaking with a small voice, and
swinging on his heels to launch and emphasise an argument. When he began a discussion, he could not bear
to leave it off, but would pick the subject to the bone,
without once relinquishing a point. An engineer by
trade, Mackay believed in the unlimited perfectibility
of all machines except the human machine. The latter
he gave up with ridicule for a compound of carrion and

perverse gases. He had an appetite for disconnected
facts which I can only compare to the savage taste for
beads. What is called information was indeed a passion
with the man, and he not only delighted to receive it,
but could pay you back in kind.

With all these capabilities, here was Mackay, already
no longer young, on his way to a new country, with no
prospects, no money, and but little hope. He was
almost tedious in the cynical disclosures of his despair.
" The ship may go down for me," he would say, " now
or to-morrow. I have nothing to lose and nothing to
hope." And again: " I am sick of the whole damned
performance." He was, like the kind little man already
quoted, another so-called victim of the bottle. But
Mackay was miles from publishing his weakness to the
world; laid the blame of his failure on corrupt masters
and a corrupt State policy; and after he had been one
night overtaken and had played the buffoon in his cups,
sternly, though not without tact, suppressed all reference to his escapade. It was a treat to see him manage
this; the various jesters withered under his gaze, and
you were forced to recognise in him a certain steely
force, and a gift of command which might have ruled
a senate.

In truth it was not whisky that had ruined him; he
was ruined long before for all good human purposes
but conversation. His eyes were sealed by a cheap,
school-book materialism. He could see nothing in the
world but money and steam-engines. He did not know
what you meant by the word happiness. He had forgotten the simple emotions of childhood, and perhaps
never encountered the delights of youth. He believed
in production, that useful figment of economy, as if it
had been real like laughter; and production, without
prejudice to liquor, was his god and guide. One day he
took me to task—a novel cry to me—upon the over-

payment of literature. Literary men, he said, were more highly paid than artisans; yet the artisan made threshing-machines and butter-churns, and the man of letters, except in the way of a few useful handbooks, made nothing worth the while. He produced a mere fancy article. Mackay's notion of a book was Hoppus's *Measurer*. Now in my time I have possessed and even studied that work; but if I were to be left to-morrow on Juan Fernandez, Hoppus's is not the book that I should choose for my companion volume.

I tried to fight the point with Mackay. I made him own that he had taken pleasure in reading books otherwise, to his view, insignificant; but he was too wary to advance a step beyond the admission. It was in vain for me to argue that here was pleasure ready-made and running from the spring, whereas his ploughs and butter-churns were but means and mechanisms to give men the necessary food and leisure before they start upon the search for pleasure; he jibbed and ran away from such conclusions. The thing was different, he declared, and nothing was serviceable but what had to do with food. " Eat, eat, eat! " he cried; " that's the bottom and the top." By an odd irony of circumstance, he grew so much interested in this discussion that he let the hour slip by unnoticed and had to go without his tea. He had enough sense and humour, indeed he had no lack of either, to have chuckled over this himself in private; and even to me he referred to it with the shadow of a smile.

Mackay was a hot bigot. He would not hear of religion. I have seen him waste hours of time in argument with all sort of poor human creatures who understood neither him nor themselves, and he had had the boyishness to dissect and criticise even so small a matter as the riddler's definition of mind. He snorted aloud with zealotry and the lust for intellectual battle.

Anything, whatever it was, that seemed to him likely to discourage the continued passionate production of corn and steam-engines he resented like a conspiracy against the people. Thus, when I put in the plea for literature, that it was only in good books, or in the society of the good, that a man could get help in his conduct, he declared I was in a different world from him. " Damn my conduct! " said he. " I have given it up for a bad job. My question is, ' Can I drive a nail? ' " And he plainly looked upon me as one who was insidiously seeking to reduce the people's annual bellyful of corn and steam-engines.

It may be argued that these opinions spring from the defect of culture; that a narrow and pinching way of life not only exaggerates to a man the importance of material conditions, but indirectly, by denying him the necessary books and leisure, keeps his mind ignorant of larger thoughts; and that hence springs this over-whelming concern about diet, and hence the bald view of existence professed by Mackay. Had this been an English peasant the conclusion would be tenable. But Mackay had most of the elements of a liberal education. He had skirted metaphysical and mathematical studies. He had a thoughtful hold of what he knew, which would be exceptional among bankers. He had been brought up in the midst of hot-house piety, and told, with incongruous pride, the story of his own brother's deathbed ecstasies. Yet he had somehow failed to fulfil himself, and was adrift like a dead thing among external circumstances, without hope or lively preference or shaping aim. And further, there seemed a tendency among many of his fellows to fall into the same blank and unlovely opinions. One thing, indeed, is not to be learned in Scotland, and that is the way to be happy. Yet that is the whole of culture, and perhaps two-thirds of morality. Can it be that the Puritan school, by divorcing a man from nature, by thinning out his instincts, and setting a stamp of its disapproval on whole fields of human activity and interest, leads at last directly to material greed?

Nature is a good guide through life, and the love of simple pleasures next, if not superior, to virtue; and we had on board an Irishman who based his claim to the widest and most affectionate popularity precisely upon these two qualities, that he was natural and happy. He boasted a fresh colour, a tight little figure, unquench-able gaiety, and indefatigable goodwill. His clothes puzzled the diagnostic mind, until you heard he had been once a private coachman, when they became eloquent and seemed a part of his biography. His face contained the rest, and, I fear, a prophecy of the future; the hawk's nose above accorded so ill with the pink baby's mouth below. His spirit and his pride belonged, you might say, to the nose; while it was the general shiftlessness expressed by the other that had thrown him from situation to situation, and at length on board the emigrant ship. Barney ate, so to speak, nothing from the galley; his own tea, butter and eggs supported him throughout the voyage; and about meal-time you might often find him up to the elbows in amateur cookery. His was the first voice heard singing among all the passengers; he was the first who fell to dancing. From Loch Foyle to Sandy Hook there was not a piece of fun undertaken but there was Barney in the midst.

You ought to have seen him when he stood up to sing at our concerts—his tight little figure stepping to and fro, and his feet shuffling to the air, his eyes seeking and bestowing encouragement—and to have enjoyed the bow, so nicely calculated between jest and earnest, between grace and clumsiness, with which he brought each song to a conclusion. He was not only a great favourite among ourselves, but his songs attracted the

lords of the saloon, who often leaned to hear him over
the rails of the hurricane-deck. He was somewhat
pleased, but not at all abashed by this attention; and
one night in the midst of his famous performance of
" Billy Keogh," I saw him spin half round in a pirou-
ette and throw an audacious wink to an old gentleman
above.

This was the more characteristic, as, for all his
daffing, he was a modest and very polite little fellow
among ourselves.

He would not have hurt the feelings of a fly, nor
throughout the passage did he give a shadow of offence;
yet he was always, by his innocent freedoms and love
of fun, brought upon that narrow margin where polite-
ness must be natural to walk without a fall. He was
once seriously angry, and that in a grave, quiet manner,
because they supplied no fish on Friday; for Barney
was a conscientious Catholic. He had likewise strict
notions of refinement; and when, late one evening,
after the women had retired, a young Scotsman struck
up an indecent song, Barney's drab clothes were immediately missing from the group. His taste was for
the society of gentlemen, of whom, with the reader's
permission, there was no lack in our five steerages and
second cabin; and he avoided the rough and positive
with a girlish shrinking. Mackay, partly from his
superior powers of mind, which rendered him incom-
prehensible, partly from his extreme opinions, was
especially distasteful to the Irishman. I have seen him
slink off with backward looks of terror and offended
delicacy, while the other, in his witty, ugly way, had
been professing hostility to God, and an extreme
theatrical readiness to be shipwrecked on the spot.
These utterances hurt the little coachman's modesty
like a bad word.

One night Jones, the young O'Reilly, and myself were walking arm-in-arm and briskly up and down the deck. Six bells had rung; a head-wind blew chill and fitful, the fog was closing in with a sprinkle of rain, and the fog-whistle had been turned on, and now divided time with its unwelcome outcries, loud like a bull, thrilling and intense like a mosquito. Even the watch lay somewhere snugly out of sight.

For some time we observed something lying black and huddled in the scuppers, which at last heaved a little and moaned aloud. We ran to the rails. An elderly man, but whether passenger or seaman it was impossible in the darkness to determine, lay grovelling on his belly in the wet scuppers, and kicking feebly with his outspread toes. We asked him what was amiss, and he replied incoherently, with a strange accent and in a voice unmanned by terror, that he had cramp in the stomach, that he had been ailing all day, had seen the doctor twice, and had walked the deck against fatigue till he was overmastered and had fallen where we found him.

Jones remained by his side, while O'Reilly and I hurried off to seek the doctor. We knocked in vain at the doctor's cabin; there came no reply; nor could we find anyone to guide us. It was no time for delicacy; so we ran once more forward; and I, whipping up a ladder and touching my hat to the officer of the watch, addressed him as politely as I could:

" I beg your pardon, sir; but there is a man lying bad with cramp in the lee scuppers; and I can't find the doctor."

He looked at me peeringly in the darkness; and then, somewhat harshly, "Well, *I* can't leave the bridge, my man," said he.

"No, sir, but you can tell me what to do," I returned.

" Is it one of the crew? " he asked.

" I believe him to be a fireman," I replied.

I daresay officers are much annoyed by complaints and alarmist information from their freight of human creatures, but certainly, whether it was the idea that the sick man was one of the crew, or from something conciliatory in my address, the officer in question was immediately relieved and mollified; and, speaking in a voice much freer from constraint, advised me to find a steward and despatch him in quest of the doctor, who would now be in the smoking-room over his pipe.

One of the stewards was often enough to be found about this hour down our companion, Steerage No. 2 and 3; that was his smoking-room of a night. Let me call him Blackwood. O'Reilly and I rattled down the companion, breathing hurry; and in his shirt-sleeves and perched across the carpenter's bench upon one thigh, found Blackwood; a neat, bright, dapper, Glasgow-looking man, with a bead of an eye and a rank twang in his speech. I forget who was with him, but the pair were enjoying a deliberate talk over their pipes. I daresay he was tired with his day's work, and eminently comfortable at that moment; and the truth is, I did not stop to consider his feelings, but told my story in a breath.

" Steward," said I, " there's a man lying bad with cramp, and I can't find the doctor."

He turned upon me as pert as a sparrow, but with a black look that is the prerogative of man; and taking his pipe out of his mouth—

" That's none of my business," said he. " I don't care."

I could have strangled the little ruffian where he sat. The thought of his cabin civility and cabin tips filled me with indignation. I glanced at O'Reilly; he was pale and quivering, and looked like assault and battery, every inch of him. But we had a better card than violence.

" You will have to make it your business," said I, " for I am sent to you by the officer on the bridge."

Blackwood was fairly tripped. He made no answer, but put out his pipe, gave me one murderous look, and set off upon his errand strolling. From that day forward, I should say, he improved to me in courtesy, as though he had repented his evil speech and were anxious to leave a better impression.

When we got on deck again, Jones was still beside the sick man; and two or three late stragglers had gathered round and were offering suggestions. One proposed to give the patient water, which was promptly negatived. Another bade us hold him up; he himself prayed to be let lie; but as it was at least as well to keep him off the streaming decks, O'Reilly and I supported him between us. It was only by main force that we did so, and neither an easy nor an agreeable duty; for he fought in his paroxysms like a frightened child, and moaned miserably when he resigned himself to our control.

" O let me lie! " he pleaded. " I'll no' get better anyway." And then, with a moan that went to my heart, " O why did I come upon this miserable journey? "

I was reminded of the song which I had heard a little while before in the close, tossing steerage: " O why left I my hame? "

Meantime Jones, relieved of his immediate charge, had gone off to the galley, where he could see a light. There he found a belated cook scouring pans by the radiance of two lanterns, and one of these he sought to borrow. The scullion was backward. " Was it one of the crew? " he asked. And when Jones, smitten with my theory, had assured that it was a fireman, he reluctantly left his scouring and came towards us at an easy pace, with one of the lanterns swinging from his finger. The light, as it reached the spot, showed us an elderly man, thick-set, and grizzled with years; but the shifting and coarse shadows concealed from us the expression and even the design of his face.

So soon as the cook set eyes on him he gave a sort of whistle.

"*It's only a passenger!*" said he; and, turning about, made, lantern and all, for the galley.

"He's a man anyway," cried Jones in indignation.

"Nobody said he was a woman," said a gruff voice, which I recognised for that of the bo's'un.

All this while there was no word of Blackwood or the doctor; and now the officer came to our side of the ship and asked, over the hurricane-deck rails, if the doctor were not yet come. We told him not.

"No?" he repeated with a breathing of anger; and we saw him hurry aft in person.

Ten minutes after the doctor made his appearance deliberately enough and examined our patient with the lantern. He made little of the case, had the man brought aft to the dispensary, dosed him, and sent him forward to his bunk. Two of his neighbours in the steerage had now come to our assistance, expressing loud sorrow that such "a fine cheery body" should be sick; and these, claiming a sort of possession, took him entirely under their own care. The drug had probably relieved him, for he struggled no more, and was led along plaintive and patient, but protesting. His heart recoiled at the thought of the steerage. "O let me lie down upon the bieldy side," he cried; "O dinna take me down!" And again: "O why did ever I come upon this miserable voyage?" And yet once more, with a gasp and a wailing prolongation of the fourth word: "I had no *call* to come." But there he was; and by the doctor's orders and the kind force of his two shipmates disappeared down the companion of Steerage No. 1 into the den allotted him.

At the foot of our own companion, just where I had found Blackwood, Jones and the bo's'un were now engaged in talk. This last was a gruff, cruel-looking seaman, who must have passed near half a century upon the seas; square-headed, goat-bearded, with heavy blond eyebrows, and an eye without radiance, but inflexibly steady and hard. I had not forgotten his rough speech; but I remembered also that he had helped us about the lantern; and now seeing him in conversation with Jones, and being choked with indignation, I proceeded to blow off my steam.

"Well," said I, "I make you my compliments upon your steward," and furiously narrated what had happened.

"I've nothing to do with him," replied the bo's'un. "They're all alike. They wouldn't mind if they saw you all lying dead one upon the top of another."

This was enough. A very little humanity went a long way with me after the experience of the evening. A sympathy grew up at once between the bo's'un and myself; and that night, and during the next few days, I learned to appreciate him better. He was a remarkable type, and not at all the kind of man you find in books. He had been at Sebastopol under English colours; and again in a States ship, "after the *Alabama*, and praying God we shouldn't find her." He was a high Tory and a high Englishman. No manufacturer could have held opinions more hostile to the working man and his strikes. "The workmen," he said, "think nothing of their country. They think of nothing but themselves. They're damned greedy, selfish fellows." He would not hear of the decadence of England. "They say they send us beef from America," he

45

argued; "but who pays for it? All the money in the world's in England." The Royal Navy was the best of possible services, according to him. "Anyway, the officers are gentlemen," said he; "and you can't get hazed to death by a damned non-commissioned—— as you can in the army." Among nations, England was the first; then came France. He respected the French navy and liked the French people; and if he were forced to make a new choice in life, "by God, he would try Frenchmen!" For all his looks and rough, cold manners, I observed that children were never frightened by him; they divined him at once to be a friend; and one night when he had chalked his hand and went about stealthily setting his mark on people's clothes, it was incongruous to hear this formidable old salt chuckling over his boyish monkey trick.

In the morning, my first thought was of the sick man. I was afraid I should not recognise him, so baffling had been the light of the lantern; and found myself unable to decide if he were Scots, English, or Irish. He had certainly employed north-country words and elisions; but the accent and the pronunciation seemed unfamiliar and incongruous in my ear.

To descend on an empty stomach into Steerage No. 1, was an adventure that required some nerve. The stench was atrocious; each respiration tasted in the throat like some horrible kind of cheese; and the squalid aspect of the place was aggravated by so many people worming themselves into their clothes in the twilight of the bunks. You may guess if I was pleased, not only for him, but for myself also, when I heard that the sick man was better and had gone on deck.

The morning was raw and foggy, though the sun suffused the fog with pink and amber; the fog-horn still blew, stertorous and intermittent; and to add to the discomfort, the seamen were just beginning to wash down the decks. But for a sick man this was heaven compared to the steerage. I found him standing on the hot-water pipe, just forward of the saloon deck-house. He was smaller than I had fancied, and plain-looking; but his face was distinguished by strange and fascinating eyes, limpid grey from a distance, but, when looked into, full of changing colours and grains of gold. His manners were mild and uncompromisingly plain; and I soon saw that, when once started, he delighted to talk. His accent and language had been formed in the most natural way, since he was born in Ireland, had lived a quarter of a century on the banks of Tyne, and was married to a Scots wife. A fisherman in the season, he had fished the east coast from Fisherrow to Whitby. When the season was over, and the great boats, which required extra hands, were once drawn up on shore till the next spring, he worked as a labourer about chemical furnaces, or along the wharves unloading vessels. In this comparatively humble way of life he had gathered a competence, and could speak of his comfortable house, his hayfield, and his garden. On this ship, where so many accomplished artisans were fleeing from starvation, he was present on a pleasure trip to visit a brother in New York.

Ere he started, he informed me, he had been warned against the steerage and the steerage fare, and recommended to bring with him a ham and tea and a spice loaf. But he laughed to scorn such counsels. "*I'm* not afraid," he had told his adviser; "*I'll* get on for ten days. I've not been a fisherman for nothing." For it is no light matter, as he reminded me, to be in an open boat, perhaps waist-deep with herrings, day breaking with a scowl, and for miles on every hand lee-shores, unbroken, iron-bound, surf-beat, with only here and there an anchorage where you dare not lie, or a harbour impossible to enter with the wind that blows. The life of a North Sea fisher is one long chapter of exposure and hard work and insufficient fare; and even if he makes land at some bleak fisher port, perhaps the season is bad or his boat has been unlucky, and after fifty hours' unsleeping vigilance and toil, not a shop will give him credit for a loaf of bread. Yet the steerage of the emigrant ship had been too vile for the endurance of a man thus rudely trained. He had scarce eaten since he came on board, until the day before, when his appetite was tempted by some excellent pea-soup. We were all much of the same mind on board, and beginning with myself, had dined upon pea-soup not wisely but too well; only with him the excess had been punished, perhaps because he was weakened by former abstinence, and his first meal had resulted in a cramp. He had determined to live henceforth on biscuit; and when, two months later, he should return to England, to make the passage by saloon. The second cabin, after due inquiry, he scouted as another edition of the steerage.

He spoke apologetically of his emotion when ill. " Ye see, I had no call to be here," said he; " and I thought it was by with me last night. I've a good house at home, and plenty to nurse me, and I had no real call to leave them." Speaking of the attentions he had received from his shipmates generally, " they were all so kind," he said, " that there's none to mention." And except in so far as I might share in this, he troubled me with no reference to my services.

But what affected me in the most lively manner was the wealth of this day-labourer, paying a two months' pleasure visit to the States, and preparing to return in the saloon, and the new testimony rendered by his story, not so much to the horrors of the steerage as to the habitual comfort of the working classes. One foggy, frosty December evening I encountered on

Liberton Hill, near Edinburgh, an Irish labourer
trudging homeward from the fields. Our roads lay
together, and it was natural that we should fall into
talk. He was covered with mud; an inoffensive,
ignorant creature, who thought the Atlantic Cable was
a secret contrivance of the masters the better to oppress
labouring mankind; and I confess I was astonished to
learn that he had nearly three hundred pounds in the
bank. But this man had travelled over most of the
world, and enjoyed wonderful opportunities on some
American railroad, with two dollars a shift and double
pay on Sunday and at night; whereas my fellow-passenger had never quitted Tyneside, and had made all
that he possessed in that same accursed, down-falling
England, whence skilled mechanics, engineers, mill-
wrights, and carpenters were fleeing as from the native
country of starvation.

Fitly enough, we slid off on the subject of strikes and
wages and hard times. Being from the Tyne, and a
man who had gained and lost in his own pocket by
these fluctuations, he had much to say, and held strong
opinions on the subject. He spoke sharply of the
masters, and, when I led him on, of the men also. The
masters had been selfish and obstructive; the men
selfish, silly, and light-headed. He rehearsed to me the
course of a meeting at which he had been present, and
the somewhat long discourse which he had there pronounced, calling into question the wisdom and even
the good faith of the Union delegates; and although he
had escaped himself through flush times and starvation
times with a handsomely provided purse, he had so
little faith in either man or master, and so profound a
terror for the unerring Nemesis of mercantile affairs,
that he could think of no hope for our country outside
of a sudden and complete political subversion. Down
must go Lords and Church and Army; and capital, by

THE STOWAWAYS

On the Sunday, among a party of men who were talking in our companion, Steerage No. 2 and 3, we remarked a new figure. He wore tweed clothes, well enough made if not very fresh, and a plain smoking-cap. His face was pale, with pale eyes, and spiritedly enough designed; but though not yet thirty, a sort of black-guardly degeneration had already overtaken his features. The fine nose had grown fleshy towards the point, the pale eyes were sunk in fat. His hands were strong and elegant; his experience of life evidently varied; his speech full of pith and verve; his manners forward, but perfectly presentable. The lad who helped in the second cabin told me, in answer to a question, that he did not know who he was, but thought, " by his way of speaking, and because he was so polite, that he was some one from the saloon."

I was not so sure, for to me there was something equivocal in his air and bearing. He might have been, I thought, the son of some good family who had fallen early into dissipation and run from home. But, making every allowance, how admirable was his talk! I wish you could have heard him tell his own stories. They were so swingingly set forth, in such dramatic language, and illustrated here and there by such luminous bits of acting, that they could only lose in any reproduction. There were tales of the P. and O. Company, where he had been an officer; of the East Indies, where in former years he had lived lavishly; of the Royal Engineers, where he had served for a period; and of a dozen other sides of life, each introducing some vigorous thumb-nail portrait. He had the talk to himself that night, we were all so glad to listen. The best talkers usually address themselves to some particular society; there they are kings, elsewhere camp-followers, as a man may know Russian and yet be ignorant of

Spanish; but this fellow had a frank, headlong power of style, and a broad, human choice of subject, that would have turned any circle in the world into a circle of hearers. He was a Homeric talker, plain, strong, and cheerful; and the things and the people of which he spoke became readily and clearly present to the minds of those who heard him. This, with a certain added colouring of rhetoric and rodomontade, must have been the style of Burns, who equally charmed the ears of duchesses and hostlers.

Yet freely and personally as he spoke, many points remained obscure in his narration. The Engineers, for instance, was a service which he praised highly; it is true there would be trouble with the sergeants; but then the officers were gentlemen, and his own, in particular, one among ten thousand. It sounded so far exactly like an episode in the rakish, topsy-turvy life of such an one as I had imagined. But then there came incidents more doubtful, which showed an almost impudent greed after gratuities, and a truly impudent disregard for truth. And then there was the tale of his departure. He had wearied, it seems, of Woolwich, and one fine day, with a companion, slipped up to London for a spree. I have a suspicion that spree was meant to be a long one; but God disposes all things; and one morning, near Westminster Bridge, whom should he come across but the very sergeant who had recruited him at first! What followed? He himself indicated cavalierly that he had then resigned. Let us put it so. But these resignations are sometimes very trying.

At length, after having delighted us for hours, he took himself away from the companion; and I could ask Mackay who and what he was. " That? " said Mackay. " Why, that's one of the stowaways."

" No man," said the same authority, " who has had

anything to do with the sea would ever think of paying for a passage." I give the statement as Mackay's without endorsement; yet I am tempted to believe that it contains a grain of truth; and if you add that the man should be impudent and thievish, or else dead-broke, it may even pass for a fair representation of the facts. We gentlemen of England who live at home at ease have, I suspect, very insufficient ideas on the subject. All the world over, people are stowing away in coal-holes and dark corners, and when ships are once out to sea, appearing again, begrimed and bashful, upon deck. The career of these sea-tramps partakes largely of the adventurous. They may be poisoned by coal-gas, or die by starvation in their place of concealment; or when found they may be clapped at once and ignominiously into irons, thus to be carried to their promised land, the port of destination, and alas! brought back in the same way to that from which they started, and there delivered over to the magistrates and the seclusion of a county jail. Since I crossed the Atlantic, one miserable stowaway was found in a dying state among the fuel, uttered but a word or two, and departed for a farther country than America.

When the stowaway appears on deck, he has but one thing to pray for: that he be set to work, which is the price and sign of his forgiveness. After half an hour with a swab or a bucket, he feels himself as secure as if he had paid for his passage. It is not altogether a bad thing for the company, who get more or less efficient hands for nothing but a few plates of junk and duff; and every now and again find themselves better paid than by a whole family of cabin passengers. Not long ago, for instance, a packet was saved from nearly certain loss by the skill and courage of a stowaway engineer. As was no more than just, a handsome subscription rewarded him for his success; but even without such exceptional good fortune, as things stand in England and America, the stowaway will often make a good profit out of his adventure. Four engineers stowed away last summer on the same ship, the *Circassia* ; and before two days after their arrival each of the four had found a comfortable berth. This was the most hopeful tale of emigration that I heard from first to last; and as you see, the luck was for stowaways.

My curiosity was much inflamed by what I heard; and the next morning, as I was making the round of the ship, I was delighted to find the ex-Royal Engineer engaged in washing down the white paint of a deckhouse. There was another fellow at work beside him, a lad not more than twenty, in the most miraculous tatters, his handsome face sown with grains of beauty and lighted up by expressive eyes. Four stowaways had been found aboard our ship before she left the Clyde, but these two had alone escaped the ignominy of being put ashore. Alick, my acquaintance of last night, was Scots by birth, and by trade a practical engineer; the other was from Devonshire, and had been to sea before the mast. Two people more unlike by training, character, and habits it would be hard to imagine; yet here they were together, scrubbing paint.

Alick had held all sorts of good situations, and wasted many opportunities in life. I have heard him end a story with these words: " That was in my golden days, when I used finger-glasses." Situation after situation failed him; then followed the depression of trade, and for months he had hung round with other idlers, playing marbles all day in the West Park, and going home at night to tell his landlady how he had been seeking for a job. I believe this kind of existence was not unpleasant to Alick himself, and he might have long continued to enjoy idleness and a life on tick; but he had a comrade, let us call him Brown, who grew restive. This fellow was continually threatening to slip his cable for the States, and at last, one Wednesday, Glasgow was left widowed of her Brown. Some months afterwards, Alick met another old chum in Sauchiehall Street.

" By the by, Alick," said he, " I met a gentleman in New York who was asking for you."

" Who was that ? " asked Alick.

" The second engineer on board the *So-and-so*," was the reply.

" Well, and who is he ? "

" Brown, to be sure."

For Brown had been one of the fortunate quartette aboard the *Circassia*. If that was the way of it in the States, Alick thought it was high time to follow Brown's example. He spent his last day, as he put it, " reviewing the yeomanry," and the next morning says he to his landlady, " Mrs. X., I'll not take porridge to-day, please; I'll take some eggs."

" Why, have you found a job ? " she asked, delighted.

" Well, yes," returned the perfidious Alick; " I think I'll start to-day."

And so, well lined with eggs, start he did, but for America. I am afraid that landlady has seen the last of him.

It was easy enough to get on board in the confusion that attends a vessel's departure; and in one of the dark corners of Steerage No. 1, flat in a bunk and with an empty stomach, Alick made the voyage from the Broomielaw to Greenock. That night, the ship's yeoman pulled him out by the heels and had him before the mate. Two other stowaways had already been found and sent ashore; but by this time darkness had fallen, they were out in the middle of the estuary, and the last steamer had left them till the morning.

" Take him to the forecastle and give him a meal,"
said the mate, " and see and pack him off the first thing
to-morrow."

In the forecastle he had supper, a good night's rest,
and breakfast, and was sitting placidly with a pipe,
fancying all was over and the game up for good with
that ship, when one of the sailors grumbled out an oath
at him, with a " What are you doing there? " and " Do
you call that hiding, anyway? " There was need of no
more; Alick was in another bunk before the day was
older. Shortly before the passengers arrived, the ship
was cursorily inspected. He heard the round come
down the companion and look into one pen after
another, until they came within two of the one in which
he lay concealed. Into these last two they did not enter,
but merely glanced from without; and Alick had no
doubt that he was personally favoured in this escape.
It was the character of the man to attribute nothing to
luck and but little to kindness; whatever happened to
him, he had earned in his own right amply; favours
came to him from his singular attraction and adroitness,
and misfortunes he had always accepted with his eyes
open. Half an hour after the searchers had departed,
the steerage began to fill with legitimate passengers,
and the worst of Alick's troubles was at an end. He
was soon making himself popular, smoking other
people's tobacco and politely sharing their private
stock of delicacies, and when night came he retired to
his bunk beside the others with composure.

Next day by afternoon, Lough Foyle being already
far behind, and only the rough north-western hills of
Ireland within view, Alick appeared on deck to court
inquiry and decide his fate. As a matter of fact, he was
known to several on board, and even intimate with one
of the engineers; but it was plainly not the etiquette of
such occasions for the authorities to avow their infor-

mation. Every one professed surprise and anger on his appearance, and he was led prisoner before the captain.

" What have you got to say for yourself? " inquired the captain.

" Not much," said Alick; " but when a man has been a long time out of a job, he will do things he would not under other circumstances."

"Are you willing to work? "

Alick swore he was burning to be useful.

"And what can you do? " asked the captain.

He replied composedly that he was a brass-fitter by trade.

" I think you will be better at engineering? " suggested the officer, with a shrewd look.

" No, sir," says Alick simply.—" There's few can beat me at a lie," was his engaging commentary to me as he recounted the affair.

" Have you been to sea? " again asked the captain.

" I've had a trip on a Clyde steamboat, sir, but no more," replied the unabashed Alick.

" Well, we must try and find some work for you," concluded the officer.

And hence we behold Alick, clear of the hot engine-room, lazily scraping paint and now and then taking a pull upon a sheet. " You leave me alone," was his deduction. " When I get talking to a man, I can get round him."

The other stowaway, whom I will call the Devonian —it was noticeable that neither of them told his name —had both been brought up and seen the world in a much smaller way. His father, a confectioner, died and was closely followed by his mother. His sisters had taken, I think, to dress-making. He himself had returned from sea about a year ago and gone to live with his brother, who kept the *George Hotel*—" it was not quite a real hotel," added the candid fellow—" and had a hired man to mind the horses." At first the Devonian was very welcome; but as time went on his brother not unnaturally grew cool towards him, and he began to find himself one too many at the *George Hotel.* " I don't think brothers care much for you," he said, as a general reflection upon life. Hurt at this change, nearly penniless, and too proud to ask for more, he set off on foot and walked eighty miles to Weymouth, living on the journey as he could. He would have enlisted, but he was too small for the army and too old for the navy; and thought himself fortunate at last to find a berth on board a trading dandy. Somewhere in the Bristol Channel, the dandy sprung a leak and went down; and though the crew were picked up and brought ashore by fishermen, they found themselves with nothing but the clothes upon their back. His next engagement was scarcely better starred; for the ship proved so leaky, and frightened them all so heartily during a short passage through the Irish Sea, that the entire crew deserted and remained behind upon the quays of Belfast.

Evil days were now coming thick on the Devonian. He could find no berth in Belfast, and had to work a passage to Glasgow on a steamer. She reached the Broomielaw on a Wednesday: the Devonian had a bellyful that morning, laying in breakfast manfully to provide against the future, and set off along the quays to seek employment. But he was now not only penniless, his clothes had begun to fall in tatters; he had begun to have the look of a street Arab; and captains will have nothing to say to a ragamuffin; for in that trade, as in all others, it is the coat that depicts the man. You may hand, reef, and steer like an angel, but if you have a hole in your trousers, it is like a millstone round your neck. The Devonian lost heart at so many refusals. He had not the impudence to beg; although, as he said, " when I had money of my own, I always gave it." It was only on Saturday morning, after three whole days of starvation, that he asked a scone from a milk-woman, who added of her own accord a glass of milk. He had now made up his mind to stow away, not from any desire to see America, but merely to obtain the comfort of a place in the forecastle and a supply of familiar sea-fare. He lived by begging, always from milkwomen, and always scones and milk, and was not once refused. It was vile wet weather, and he could never have been dry. By night he walked the streets, and by day slept upon Glasgow Green, and heard, in the intervals of his dozing, the famous theologians of the spot clear up intricate points of doctrine and ap-praise the merits of the clergy. He had not much in-struction; he could " read bills on the street," but was " main bad at writing "; yet these theologians seem to have impressed him with a genuine sense of amuse-ment. Why he did not go to the Sailors' Home I know not; I presume there is in Glasgow one of these insti-tutions, which are by far the happiest and the wisest effort of contemporaneous charity; but I must stand to my author, as they say in old books, and relate the story as I heard it. In the meantime, he had tried four times to stow away in different vessels, and four times had been discovered and handed back to starvation. The fifth time was lucky; and you may judge if he were pleased to be aboard ship again, at his old work, and with duff twice a week. He was, said Alick, " a devil for the duff." Or if devil was not the word, it was one if anything stronger.

The difference in the conduct of the two was remark-able. The Devonian was as willing as any paid hand, swarmed aloft among the first, pulled his natural weight and firmly upon a rope, and found work for himself when there was none to show him. Alick, on the other hand, was not only a skulker in the grain, but took a humorous and fine gentlemanly view of the transaction. He would speak to me by the hour in ostentatious idleness; and only if the bo's'un or a mate came by, fell-to languidly for just the necessary time till they were out of sight. " I'm not breaking my heart with it," he remarked.

Once there was a hatch to be opened near where he was stationed; he watched the preparations for a second or so suspiciously, and then, " Hullo," said he, " here's some real work coming—I'm off," and he was gone that moment. Again, calculating the six guinea passage-money, and the probable duration of the passage, he remarked pleasantly that he was getting six shillings a day for this job, " and it's pretty dear to the company at that." " They are asking nothing by me," was another of his observations; " they're making something by that fellow." And he pointed to the Devonian, who was just then busy to the eyes.

The more you saw of Alick, the more, it must be owned, you learned to despise him. His natural talents were of no use either to himself or others; for his character had degenerated like his face, and become pulpy and pretentious. Even his power of persuasion, which was certainly very surprising, stood in some danger of being lost or neutralised by over-confidence. He lied in an aggressive, brazen manner, like a pert criminal in the dock; and he was so vain of his own cleverness that he could not refrain from boasting, ten minutes after, of the very trick by which he had deceived you. " Why, now I have more money than when I came on board," he said one night, exhibiting a sixpence, " and yet I stood myself a bottle of beer before I went to bed yesterday. And as for tobacco, I have fifteen sticks of it." That was fairly successful indeed; yet a man of his superiority, and with a less obtrusive policy, might, who knows? have got the length of half a crown. A man who prides himself upon persuasion should learn the persuasive faculty of silence, above all as to his own misdeeds. It is only in the farce and for dramatic purposes that Scapin enlarges on his peculiar talents to the world at large.

Scapin is perhaps a good name for this clever, unfortunate Alick; for at the bottom of all his misconduct there was a guiding sense of humour that moved you to forgive him. It was more than half as a jest that he conducted his existence. " Oh, man," he said to me once with unusual emotion, like a man thinking of his mistress, " I would give up anything for a lark."

It was in relation to his fellow-stowaway that Alick showed the best, or perhaps I should say the only, good points of his nature. " Mind you," he said suddenly, changing his tone, " mind you that's a good boy. He wouldn't tell you a lie. A lot of them think he is a scamp because his clothes are ragged, but he isn't; he's as good as gold." To hear him, you became aware that Alick himself had a taste for virtue. He thought his own idleness and the other's industry equally becoming. He was no more anxious to insure his own reputation as a liar than to uphold the truthfulness of his companion; and he seemed unaware of what was incongruous in his attitude, and was plainly sincere in both characters.

It was not surprising that he should take an interest in the Devonian, for the lad worshipped and served him in love and wonder. Busy as he was, he would find time to warn Alick of an approaching officer, or even to tell him that the coast was clear, and he might slip off and smoke a pipe in safety. " Tom," he once said to him, for that was the name which Alick ordered him to use, " if you don't like going to the galley, I'll go for you. You ain't used to this kind of thing, you ain't.

But I'm a sailor; and I can understand the feelings of any fellow, I can." Again, he was hard up, and casting about for some tobacco, for he was not so liberally used in this respect as others perhaps less worthy, when Alick offered him the half of one of his fifteen sticks. I think, for my part, he might have increased the offer to a whole one, or perhaps a pair of them, and not lived to regret his liberality. But the Devonian refused. "No," he said, "you're a stowaway like me; I won't take it from you, I'll take it from some one who's not down on his luck."

It was notable in this generous lad that he was strongly under the influence of sex. If a woman passed near where he was working, his eyes lit up, his hand paused, and his mind wandered instantly to other thoughts. It was natural that he should exercise a fascination proportionally strong upon women. He begged, you will remember, from women only, and was never refused. Without wishing to explain away the charity of those who helped him, I cannot but fancy he may have owed a little to his handsome face, and to that quick, responsive nature, formed for love, which speaks eloquently through all disguises, and can stamp an impression in ten minutes' talk or an exchange of glances. He was the more dangerous in that he was far from bold, but seemed to woo in spite of himself, and with a soft and pleading eye. Ragged as he was, and many a scarecrow is in that respect more comfortably furnished, even on board he was not without some curious admirers.

There was a girl among the passengers, a tall, blonde, handsome, strapping Irishwoman, with a wild, accommodating eye, whom Alick had dubbed Tommy, with that transcendental appropriateness that defies analysis. One day the Devonian was lying for warmth in the upper stoke-hole, which stands open on the deck, when Irish Tommy came past, very neatly attired, as was her custom.

" Poor fellow," she said, stopping, " you haven't a vest."

" No," he said; " I wish I 'ad."

Then she stood and gazed on him in silence, until, in his embarrassment, for he knew not how to look under this scrutiny, he pulled out his pipe and began to fill it with tobacco.

" Do you want a match? " she asked. And before he had time to reply, she ran off and presently returned with more than one.

That was the beginning and the end, as far as our passage is concerned, of what I will make bold to call this love-affair. There are many relations which go on to marriage and last during a lifetime, in which less human feeling is engaged than in this scene of five minutes at the stoke-hole.

Rigidly speaking, this would end the chapter of the stowaways; but in a larger sense of the word I have yet more to add. Jones had discovered and pointed out to me a young woman who was remarkable among her fellows for a pleasing and interesting air. She was poorly clad, to the verge, if not over the line, of disrespectability, with a ragged old jacket and a bit of a sealskin cap no bigger than your fist; but her eyes, her whole expression, and her manner, even in ordinary moments, told of a true womanly nature, capable of love, anger, and devotion. She had a look, too, of refinement, like one who might have been a better lady than most, had she been allowed the opportunity. When alone she seemed preoccupied and sad; but she was not often alone; there was usually by her side a heavy, dull, gross man in rough clothes, chary of speech and gesture—not from caution, but poverty of disposition; a man like a ditcher, unlovely and uninteresting; whom she petted and tended and waited on with her eyes as if he had been Amadis of Gaul. It was strange to see this hulking fellow dog-sick, and this delicate, sad woman caring for him. He seemed, from first to last, insensible of her caresses and attentions, and she seemed unconscious of his insensibility. The Irish husband, who sang his wife to sleep, and this Scottish girl serving her Orson, were the two bits of human nature that most appealed to me throughout the voyage.

On the Thursday before we arrived, the tickets were collected; and soon a rumour began to go round the vessel; and this girl, with her bit of sealskin cap, became the centre of whispering and pointed fingers. She also, it was said, was a stowaway of a sort; for she was on board with neither ticket nor money; and the man with whom she travelled was the father of a family, who had left wife and children to be hers. The ship's officers discouraged the story, which may therefore have been a story and no more; but it was believed in the steerage, and the poor girl had to encounter many curious eyes from that day forth.

PERSONAL EXPERIENCE AND REVIEW

Travel is of two kinds; and this voyage of mine across the ocean combined both. " Out of my country and myself I go," sings the old poet; and I was not only travelling out of my country in latitude and longitude, but out of myself in diet, associates, and consideration. Part of the interest and a great deal of the amusement flowed, at least to me, from this novel situation in the world.

I found that I had what they call fallen in life with absolute success and verisimilitude. I was taken for a steerage passenger; no one seemed surprised that I should be so; and there was nothing but the brass plate between decks to remind me that I had once been a gentleman. In a former book, describing a former journey, I expressed some wonder that I could be readily and naturally taken for a pedlar, and explained the accident by the difference of language and manners between England and France. I must now take a humbler view; for here I was among my own country-men, somewhat roughly clad, to be sure, but with every advantage of speech and manner; and I am bound to confess that I passed for nearly anything you please except an educated gentleman. The sailors called me " mate," the officers addressed me as " my man," my comrades accepted me without hesitation for a person of their own character and experience, but with some curious information. One, a mason himself, believed I was a mason; several, and among these at least one of the seamen, judged me to be a petty officer in the American navy; and I was so often set down for a prac-tical engineer that at last I had not the heart to deny it. From all these guesses I drew one conclusion, which told against the insight of my companions. They might be close observers in their own way, and read the manners in the face; but it was plain that they did not extend their observation to the hands.

To the saloon passengers also I sustained my part without a hitch. It is true I came little in their way; but when we did encounter, there was no recognition in their eye, although I confess I sometimes courted it in silence. All these, my inferiors and equals, took me, like the transformed monarch in the story, for a mere common, human man. They gave me a hard, dead look, with the flesh about the eye kept unrelaxed.

With the women this surprised me less, as I had already experimented on the sex by going abroad through a suburban part of London simply attired in a sleeve-waistcoat. The result was curious. I then learned for the first time, and by the exhaustive process, how much attention ladies are accustomed to bestow on all male creatures of their own station; for, in my humble rig, each one who went by me caused me a certain shock of surprise and a sense of something wanting. In my normal circumstances, it appeared every young lady must have paid me some tribute of a glance; and though I had often not detected it when it was given, I was well aware of its absence when it was withheld. My height seemed to decrease with every woman who passed me, for she passed me like a dog. This is one of my grounds for supposing that what are called the upper classes may sometimes produce a disagreeable impression in what are called the lower; and I wish some one would continue my experiment, and find out exactly at what stage of toilette a man becomes invisible to the well-regulated female eye.

Here on shipboard the matter was put to a more complete test; for, even with the addition of speech and manner, I passed among the ladies for precisely the average man of the steerage. It was one afternoon that I saw this demonstrated. A very plainly dressed woman was taken ill on deck. I think I had the luck to be present at every sudden seizure during all the passage; and on this occasion found myself in the place of importance, supporting the sufferer. There was not only a large crowd immediately around us, but a considerable knot of saloon passengers leaning over our heads from the hurricane deck. One of these, an elderly managing woman, hailed me with counsels. Of course I had to reply; and as the talk went on, I began to discover that the whole group took me for the husband. I looked upon my new wife, poor creature, with mingled feelings; and I must own she had not even the appearance of the poorest class of city servant-maids, but looked more like a country wench, who should have been employed at a roadside inn. Now was the time for me to go and study the brass plate.

To such of the officers as knew about me—the doctor, the purser, and the stewards—I appeared in the light of a broad joke. The fact that I spent the better part of my day in writing had gone abroad over the ship and tickled them all prodigiously. Whenever they met me they referred to my absurd occupation with familiarity and breadth of humorous intention. Their manner was well calculated to remind me of my fallen fortunes. You may be sincerely amused by the amateur literary efforts of a gentleman, but you scarce publish the feeling to his face. "Well!" they would say: "still writing?" And the smile would widen into a laugh. The purser came one day into the cabin, and, touched to the heart by my misguided industry, offered me some other kind of writing, "for which," he added pointedly, "you will be paid." This was nothing else than to copy out the list of passengers.

Another trick of mine which told against my reputation was my choice of roosting-place in an active draught upon the cabin floor. I was openly jeered and flouted for this eccentricity; and a considerable knot would sometimes gather at the door to see my last dispositions for the night. This was embarrassing, but I learned to support the trial with equanimity.

Indeed, I may say that, upon the whole, my new position sat lightly and naturally upon my spirits. I accepted the consequences with readiness, and found them far from difficult to bear. The steerage conquered me; I conformed more and more to the type of the place, not only in manner but at heart, growing hostile to the officers and cabin passengers who looked down upon me, and day by day greedier for small delicacies. Such was the result, as I fancy, of a diet of bread and butter, soup and porridge. We think we have no sweet tooth as long as we are full to the brim of molasses; but a man must have sojourned in the workhouse before he boasts himself indifferent to dainties. Every evening, for instance, I was more and more preoccupied about our doubtful fare at tea. If it was delicate my heart was much lightened; if it was but broken fish I was proportionally downcast. The offer of a little jelly from a fellow-passenger more provident than myself caused a marked elevation in my spirits. And I would have gone to the ship's end and back again for an oyster or a chipped fruit.

In other ways I was content with my position. It seemed no disgrace to be confounded with my company; for I may as well declare at once I found their manners as gentle and becoming as those of any other class. I do not mean that my friends could have sat down without embarrassment and laughable disaster at the table of a duke. That does not imply an inferiority of breeding, but a difference of usage. Thus I flatter myself that I conducted myself well among my fellow-passengers; yet my most ambitious hope is not to have avoided faults, but to have committed as few as possible. I know too well that my tact is not the same as their tact, and that my habit of a different society constituted, not only no qualification, but a positive disability to move easily and becomingly in this. When Jones complimented me—because I " managed to behave very pleasantly " to my fellow-passengers, was how he put it—I could follow the thought in his mind, and knew his compliment to be such as we pay foreigners on their proficiency in English. I dare say this praise was given me immediately on the back of some unpardonable solecism, which had led him to review my conduct as a whole. We are all ready to laugh at the ploughman among lords; we should consider also the case of a lord among the ploughmen. I have seen a lawyer in the house of a Hebridean fisherman; and I know, but nothing will induce me to disclose, which of these two was the better gentleman. Some of our finest behaviour, though it looks well enough from the boxes, may seem even brutal to the gallery. We boast too often manners that are parochial rather than universal; that, like a country wine, will not bear transportation for a hundred miles, nor from the parlour to the kitchen. To be a gentleman is to be one all the world over, and in every relation and grade of society. It is a high calling, to which a man must first be born, and then devote himself for life. And, unhappily, the manners of a certain so-called upper grade have a kind of currency, and meet with a certain external acceptation throughout all the others, and this tends to keep us well satisfied with slight acquirements and the amateurish accomplishments of a clique. But manners, like art, should be human and central.

Some of my fellow-passengers, as I now moved among them in a relation of equality, seemed to me excellent gentlemen. They were not rough, nor hasty, nor disputatious; debated pleasantly, differed kindly;

were helpful, gentle, patient, and placid. The type of manners was plain, and even heavy; there was little to please the eye, but nothing to shock; and I thought gentleness lay more nearly at the spring of behaviour than in many more ornate and delicate societies. I say delicate, where I cannot say refined; a thing may be fine like ironwork, without being delicate like lace. There was here less delicacy; the skin supported more callously the natural surface of events, the mind received more bravely the crude facts of human existence; but I do not think that there was less effective refinement, less consideration for others, less polite suppression of self. I speak of the best among my fellow-passengers; for in the steerage, as well as in the saloon, there is a mixture. Those, then, with whom I found myself in sympathy, and of whom I may therefore hope to write with a greater measure of truth, were not only as good in their manners, but endowed with very much the same natural capacities, and about as wise in deduction, as the bankers and barristers of what is called society. One and all were too much interested in disconnected facts, and loved information for its own sake with too rash a devotion; but people in all classes display the same appetite as they gorge themselves daily with the miscellaneous gossip of the newspaper. Newspaper reading, as far as I can make out, is often rather a sort of brown study than an act of culture. I have myself palmed off yesterday's issue on a friend, and seen him re-peruse it for a continuance of minutes with an air at once refreshed and solemn. Workmen, perhaps, pay more attention; but though they may be eager listeners, they have rarely seemed to me either willing or careful thinkers. Culture is not measured by the greatness of the field which is covered by our knowledge, but by the nicety with which we can perceive relations in that field, whether great or small. Workmen, certainly those who were on board with me, I found wanting in this quality or habit of the mind. They did not perceive relations, but leaped to a so-called cause, and thought the problem settled. Thus the cause of everything in England was the form of government, and the cure for all evils was, by consequence, a revolution. It is surprising how many of them said this, and that none should have had a definite thought in his head as he said it. Some hated the Church because they disagreed with it; some hated Lord Beaconsfield because of war and taxes; all hated the masters, possibly with reason. But these feelings were not at the root of the matter; the true reasoning of their souls ran thus—I have not got on; I ought to have got on; if there was a revolution I should get on. How? They had no idea. Why? Because—because—well, look at America!

To be politically blind is no distinction; we are all so, if you come to that. At bottom, as it seems to me, there is but one question in modern home politics, though it appears in many shapes, and that is the question of money; and but one political remedy, that the people should grow wiser and better. My workmen fellow-passengers were as impatient and dull of hearing on the second of these points as any member of Parliament; but they had some glimmerings of the first. They would not hear of improvement on their part, but wished the world made over again in a crack, so that they might remain improvident and idle and debauched, and yet enjoy the comfort and respect that should accompany the opposite virtues; and it was in this expectation, as far as I could see, that many of them were now on their way to America. But on the point of money they saw clearly enough that inland politics, so far as they were concerned, were reducible to the question of annual income; a question which should long ago have been settled by a revolution, they did not know how, and which they were now about to settle for themselves, once more they knew not how, by crossing the Atlantic in a steamship of considerable tonnage.

And yet it has been amply shown them that the second or income question is in itself nothing, and may as well be left undecided, if there be no wisdom and virtue to profit by the change. It is not by a man's purse, but by his character, that he is rich or poor. Barney will be poor, Alick will be poor, Mackay will be poor; let them go where they will, and wreck all the governments under heaven, they will be poor until they die.

Nothing is perhaps more notable in the average workman than his surprising idleness, and the candour with which he confesses to the failing. It has to me been always something of a relief to find the poor, as a general rule, so little oppressed with work. I can in consequence enjoy my own more fortunate beginning with a better grace. The other day I was living with a farmer in America, an old frontiersman, who had worked and fought, hunted and farmed, from his childhood up. He excused himself for his defective education on the ground that he had been overworked from first to last. Even now, he said, anxious as he was, he had never the time to take up a book. In consequence of this, I observed him closely; he was occupied for four or, at the extreme outside, for five hours out of the twenty-four, and then principally in walking; and the remainder of the day he passed in born idleness, either eating fruit or standing with his back against a door. I have known men do hard literary work all morning, and then undergo quite as much physical fatigue by way of relief as satisfied this powerful frontiersman for the day. He, at least, like all the educated class, did so

72

much homage to industry as to persuade himself he was industrious. But the average mechanic recognises his idleness with effrontery; he has even, as I am told, organised it.

I give the story as it was told me, and it was told me for a fact. A man fell from a housetop in the city of Aberdeen, and was brought into hospital with broken bones. He was asked what was his trade, and replied that he was a *tapper*. No one had ever heard of such a thing before; the officials were filled with curiosity; they besought an explanation. It appeared that when a party of slaters were engaged upon a roof, they would now and then be taken with a fancy for the public-house. Now a seamstress, for example, might slip away from her work and no one be the wiser; but if these fellows adjourned, the tapping of the mallets would cease, and thus the neighbourhood be advertised of their defection. Hence the career of the tapper. He has to do the tapping and keep up an industrious bustle on the housetop during the absence of the slaters. When he taps for only one or two the thing is child's-play, but when he has to represent a whole troop, it is then that he earns his money in the sweat of his brow. Then must he bound from spot to spot, reduplicate, triplicate, sextuplicate his single personality, and swell and hasten his blows, until he produce a perfect illusion for the ear, and you would swear that a crowd of emulous masons were continuing merrily to roof the house. It must be a strange sight from an upper window.

I heard nothing on board of the tapper; but I was astonished at the stories told by my companions. Skulking, shirking, malingering, were all established tactics, it appeared. They could see no dishonesty where a man who is paid for an hour's work gives half an hour's consistent idling in its place. Thus the tapper

73

would refuse to watch for the police during a burglary, and call himself an honest man. It is not sufficiently recognised that our race detests to work. If I thought that I should have to work every day of my life as hard as I am working now, I should be tempted to give up the struggle. And the workman early begins on his career of toil. He has never had his fill of holidays in the past, and his prospect of holidays in the future is both distant and uncertain. In the circumstances, it would require a high degree of virtue not to snatch alleviations for the moment.

There were many good talkers on the ship; and I believe good talking of a certain sort is a common accomplishment among working men. Where books are comparatively scarce, a greater amount of information will be given and received by word of mouth; and this tends to produce good talkers, and, what is no less needful for conversation, good listeners. They could all tell a story with effect. I am sometimes tempted to think that the less literary class show always better in narration; they have so much more patience with detail, are so much less hurried to reach the points, and preserve so much juster a proportion among the facts. At the same time their talk is dry; they pursue a topic ploddingly, have not an agile fancy, do not throw sudden lights from unexpected quarters, and when the talk is over they often leave the matter where it was. They mark time instead of marching. They think only to argue, not to reach new conclusions, and use their reason rather as a weapon of offence than as a tool for self-improvement. Hence the talk of some of the cleverest was unprofitable in result, because there was no give and take; they would grant you as little as possible for premise, and begin to dispute under an oath to conquer or to die.

But the talk of a workman is apt to be more interesting than that of a wealthy merchant, because the thoughts, hopes, and fears of which the workman's life is built lie nearer to necessity and nature. They are more immediate to human life. An income calculated by the week is a far more human thing than one calculated by the year, and a small income, simply from its smallness, than a large one. I never wearied listening to the details of a workman's economy, because every item stood for some real pleasure. If he could afford pudding twice a week, you know that twice a week the man ate with genuine gusto and was physically happy; while if you learn that a rich man has seven courses a day, ten to one the half of them remain untasted, and the whole is but misspent money and a weariness to the flesh.

The difference between England and America to a working man was thus most humanly put to me by a fellow-passenger: " In America," said he, " you get pies and puddings." I do not hear enough, in economy books, of pies and puddings. A man lives in and for the delicacies, adornments, and accidental attributes of life, such as pudding to eat and pleasant books and theatres to occupy his leisure. The bare terms of existence would be rejected with contempt by all. If a man feeds on bread and butter, soup and porridge, his appetite grows wolfish after dainties. And the workman dwells in a borderland, and is always within sight of those cheerless regions where life is more difficult to sustain than worth sustaining. Every detail of our existence, where it is worth while to cross the ocean after pie and pudding, is made alive and enthralling by the presence of genuine desire; but it is all one to me whether Crœsus has a hundred or a thousand thousands in the bank. There is more adventure in the life of the working man who descends as a common soldier into the battle of life, than in that of the millionaire who sits

75

NEW YORK

As we drew near to New York I was at first amused, and then somewhat staggered, by the cautious and the grisly tales that went the round. You would have thought we were to land upon a cannibal island. You must speak to no one in the streets, as they would not leave you till you were rooked and beaten. You must enter an hotel with military precautions; for the least you had to apprehend was to awake next morning without money or baggage, or necessary raiment, a lone forked radish in a bed; and if the worst befell, you would instantly and mysteriously disappear from the ranks of mankind.

I have usually found such stories correspond to the least modicum of fact. Thus I was warned, I remember, against the roadside inns of the Cevennes, and that by a learned professor; and when I reached Pradelles the warning was explained; it was but the far-away rumour and reduplication of a single terrifying story already half a century old, and half forgotten in the theatre of the events. So I was tempted to make light of these reports against America. But we had on board with us a man whose evidence it would not do to put aside. He had come near these perils in the body; he had visited a robber inn. The public has an old and well-grounded favour for this class of incident, and shall be gratified to the best of my power.

My fellow-passenger, whom we shall call M'Naughten, had come from New York to Boston with a comrade, seeking work. They were a pair of rattling blades; and, leaving their baggage at the station, passed the day in beer-saloons, and with congenial spirits, until midnight struck. Then they applied themselves to find a lodging, and walked the streets till two, knocking at houses of entertainment and being refused admittance, or themselves declining the terms. By two the inspiration of their liquor had begun to wear off; they were weary and humble, and after a great circuit found themselves in the same street where they had begun their search, and in front of a French hotel where they had already sought accommodation. Seeing the house still open, they returned to the charge. A man in a white cap sat in an office by the door. He seemed to welcome them more warmly than when they had first presented themselves, and the charge for the night had somewhat unaccountably fallen from a dollar to a quarter. They thought him ill-looking, but paid their quarter apiece, and were shown upstairs to the top of the house. There, in a small room, the man in the white cap wished them pleasant slumbers.

It was furnished with a bed, a chair, and some conveniences. The door did not lock on the inside; and the only sign of adornment was a couple of framed pictures, one close above the head of the bed, and the other opposite the foot, and both curtained, as we may sometimes see valuable water-colours, or the portraits of the dead, or works of art more than usually skittish in the subject. It was perhaps in the hope of finding something of this last description that M'Naughten's comrade pulled aside the curtain of the first. He was startlingly disappointed. There was no picture. The frame surrounded, and the curtain was designed to hide, an oblong aperture in the partition, through which they looked forth into the dark corridor. A person standing without could easily take a purse from under the pillow, or even strangle a sleeper as he lay abed. M'Naughten and his comrade stared at each other like Balboa and his men, " with a wild surmise "; and then the latter, catching up the lamp, ran to the other frame and roughly raised the curtain. There he stood, petrified; and M'Naughten, who had followed, grasped him by the wrist in terror. They could see into another room, larger in size than that which they occupied, where three men sat crouching and silent in the dark. For a second or so these five persons looked each other in the eyes, then the curtain was dropped, and M'Naughten and his friend made but one bolt of it out of the room and downstairs. The man in the white cap said nothing as they passed him; and they were so pleased to be once more in the open night that they gave up all notion of a bed, and walked the streets of Boston till the morning.

No one seemed much cast down by these stories, but all inquired after the address of a respectable hotel; and I, for my part, put myself under the conduct of Mr. Jones. Before noon of the second Sunday we sighted the low shores outside of New York harbour; the steerage passengers must remain on board to pass through Castle Garden on the following morning; but we of the second cabin made our escape along with the lords of the saloon; and by six o'clock Jones and I issued into West Street, sitting on some straw in the bottom of an open baggage-wagon. It rained miraculously; and from that moment till on the following night I left New York, there was scarce a lull, and no cessation of the downpour. The roadways were flooded; a loud strident noise of falling water filled the air; the restaurants smelt heavily of wet people and wet clothing.

It took us but a few minutes, though it cost us a good deal of money, to be rattled along West Street to our destination: "Reunion House, No. 10 West Street, one minute's walk from Castle Garden; convenient to Castle Garden, the Steamboat Landings, California Steamers and Liverpool Ships; Board and Lodging per day 1 dollar, single meals 25 cents, lodging per night 25 cents; private rooms for families; no charge for storage or baggage; satisfaction guaranteed to all persons; Michael Mitchell, Proprietor." Reunion House was, I may go the length of saying, a humble hostelry. You entered through a long bar-room, thence passed into a little dining-room, and thence into a still smaller kitchen. The furniture was of the plainest; but the bar was hung in the American taste, with encouraging and hospitable mottoes.

Jones was well known; we were received warmly; and two minutes afterwards I had refused a drink from the proprietor, and was going on, in my plain European fashion, to refuse a cigar, when Mr. Mitchell sternly interposed, and explained the situation. He was offering to treat me, it appeared; whenever an American bar-keeper proposes anything it must be borne in mind that he is offering to treat; and if I did not want a drink, I must at least take the cigar. I took it bashfully, feeling I had begun my American career on the wrong foot. I did not enjoy that cigar; but this may have been from a variety of reasons, even the best cigar often failing to please if you smoke three-quarters of it in a drenching rain.

For many years America was to me a sort of promised land. " Westward the march of empire holds its way "; the race is for the moment to the young; what has been and what is we imperfectly and obscurely know; what is to be yet lies beyond the flight of our imaginations. Greece, Rome and Judæa are gone by for ever, leaving to generations the legacy of their accomplished work; China still endures, an old-inhabited house in the brand-new city of nations; England has already declined, since she has lost the States; and to these States, therefore, yet undeveloped, full of dark possibilities, and grown, like another Eve, from one rib out of the side of their own old land, the minds of young men in England turn naturally at a certain hopeful period of their age. It will be hard for an

American to understand the spirit. But let him imagine a young man, who shall have grown up in an old and rigid circle, following bygone fashions and taught to distrust his own fresh instincts, and who now suddenly hears of a family of cousins, all about his own age, who keep house together by themselves and live far from restraint and tradition; let him imagine this, and he will have some imperfect notion of the sentiment with which spirited English youths turn to the thought of the American Republic. It seems to them as if, out west, the war of life was still conducted in the open air, and on free barbaric terms; as if it had not yet been narrowed into parlours, nor begun to be conducted, like some unjust and dreary arbitration, by compromise, costume, forms of procedure, and sad, senseless self-denial. Which of these two he prefers, a man with any youth still left in him will decide rightly for himself. He would rather be homeless than denied a passkey; rather go without food than partake of a stalled ox in stiff, respectable society; rather be shot out of hand than direct his life according to the dictates of the world.

He knows or thinks nothing of the Maine Laws, the Puritan sourness, the fierce, sordid appetite for dollars, or the dreary existence of country towns. A few wild story-books which delighted his childhood form the imaginative basis of his picture of America. In course of time, there is added to this a great crowd of stimulating details—vast cities that grow up as by enchantment; the birds, that have gone south in autumn, returning with the spring to find thousands camped upon their marshes, and the lamps burning far and near along populous streets; forests that disappear like snow; countries larger than Britain that are cleared and settled, one man running forth with his household gods before another, while the bear and the Indian are yet scarce aware of their approach; oil that gushes from the earth; gold that is washed or quarried in the brooks or glens of the Sierras; and all that bustle, courage, action, and constant kaleidoscopic change that Walt Whitman has seized and set forth in his vigorous, cheerful, and loquacious verses.

Here I was at last in America, and was soon out upon New York streets, spying for things foreign. The place had to me an air of Liverpool; but such was the rain that not Paradise itself would have looked inviting. We were a party of four, under two umbrellas; Jones and I and two Scots lads, recent immigrants, and not indisposed to welcome a compatriot. They had been six weeks in New York, and neither of them had yet found a single job or earned a single halfpenny. Up to the present they were exactly out of pocket by the amount of the fare.

The lads soon left us. Now I had sworn by all my gods to have such a dinner as would rouse the dead; there was scarce any expense at which I should have hesitated; the devil was in it but Jones and I should dine like heathen emperors. I set to work, asking after a restaurant; and I chose the wealthiest and most gastronomical-looking passers-by to ask from. Yet, although I had told them I was willing to pay anything in reason, one and all sent me off to cheap, fixed-price houses, where I would not have eaten that night for the cost of twenty dinners. I do not know if this were characteristic of New York, or whether it was only Jones and I who looked unfriendly and discouraged enterprising suggestions. But at length, by our own sagacity, we found a French restaurant, where there was a French waiter, some fair French cooking, some so-called French wine, and French coffee to conclude the whole. I never entered into the feelings of Jack on land so completely as when I tasted that coffee.

The Clyde to Sandy Hook

I suppose we had one of the " private rooms for families " at Reunion House. It was very small, furnished with a bed, a chair, and some clothes-pegs; and it derived all that was necessary for the life of the human animal through two borrowed lights: one looking into the passage, and the second opening, without sash, into another apartment, where three men fitly snored, or in intervals of wakefulness, drearily mumbled to each other all night long. It will be observed that this was almost exactly the disposition of the room in M'Naughten's story. Jones had the bed; I pitched my camp upon the floor; he did not sleep until near morning, and I, for my part, never closed an eye.

At sunrise I heard a cannon fired; and shortly afterwards the men in the next room gave over snoring for good, and began to rustle over their toilettes. The sound of their voices as they talked was low and moaning, like that of people watching by the sick. Jones, who had at last begun to doze, tumbled and murmured, and every now and then opened unconscious eyes upon me where I lay. I found myself growing eerier and eerier, for I daresay I was a little fevered by my restless night, and hurried to dress and get downstairs.

You had to pass through the rain, which still fell thick and resonant, to reach a lavatory on the other side of the court. There were three basin-stands, and a few crumpled towels and pieces of wet soap, white and slippery like fish; nor should I forget a looking-glass and a pair of questionable combs. Another Scots lad was here, scrubbing his face with a good will. He had been three months in New York and had not yet found a single job nor earned a single halfpenny. Up to the present, he also was exactly out of pocket by the amount of the fare. I began to grow sick at heart for my fellow-emigrants.

Of my nightmare wanderings in New York I spare

83

to tell. I had a thousand and one things to do; only the day to do them in, and a journey across the continent before me in the evening. It rained with patient fury; every now and then I had to get under cover for a while in order, so to speak, to give my mackintosh a rest; for under this continued drenching it began to grow damp on the inside. I went to banks, post-offices, railway-offices, restaurants, publishers, booksellers, money-changers, and wherever I went a pool would gather about my feet, and those who were careful of their floors would look on with an unfriendly eye. Wherever I went, too, the same traits struck me : the people were all surprisingly rude and surprisingly kind. The money-changer cross-questioned me like a French commissary, asking my age, my business, my average income, and my destination, beating down my attempts at evasion, and receiving my answers in silence; and yet when all was over, he shook hands with me up to the elbows, and sent his lad nearly a quarter of a mile in the rain to get me books at a reduction. Again, in a very large publishing and bookselling establishment a man, who seemed to be the manager, received me as I had certainly never before been received in any human shop, indicated squarely that he put no faith in my honesty, and refused to look up the names of books or give me the slightest help of information, on the ground, like the steward, that it was none of his business. I lost my temper at last, said I was a stranger in America and not learned in their etiquette; but I would assure him, if he went to any bookseller in England, of more handsome usage. The boast was perhaps exaggerated; but like many a long shot, it struck the gold. The manager passed at once from one extreme to the other; I may say that from that moment he loaded me with kindness; he gave me all sorts of good advice, wrote me down addresses, and came bareheaded into the rain to point me out a restaurant, where I might lunch, nor even then did he seem to think that he had done enough. These are (it is as well to be bold in statement) the manners of America. It is this same opposition that has most struck me in people of almost all classes and from east to west. By the time a man had about strung me up to be the death of him by his insulting behaviour, he himself would be just upon the point of melting into confidence and serviceable attention. Yet I suspect, although I have met with the like in so many parts, that this must be the character of some particular State or group of States; for in America, and this again in all classes, you will find some of the softest-mannered gentlemen in the world.

I was so wet when I got back to Mitchell's towards the evening, that I had simply to divest myself of my shoes, socks and trousers, and leave them behind for the benefit of New York City. No fire could have dried them ere I had to start; and to pack them in their present condition was to spread ruin among my other possessions. With a heavy heart I said farewell to them as they lay a pulp in the middle of a pool upon the floor of Mitchell's kitchen. I wonder if they are dry by now. Mitchell hired a man to carry my baggage to the station, which was hard by, accompanied me thither himself, and recommended me to the particular attention of the officials. No one could have been kinder. Those who are out of pocket may go safely to Reunion House, where they will get decent meals and find an honest and obliging landlord. I owed him this word of thanks, before I enter fairly on the second and far less agreeable chapter of my emigrant experience.

PART II
ACROSS THE PLAINS

LEAVES FROM THE NOTEBOOK OF AN EMIGRANT
BETWEEN NEW YORK AND SAN FRANCISCO

DEDICATORY NOTE
TO
"ACROSS THE PLAINS"

TO
PAUL BOURGET

Traveller and student and curious as you are, you will never have heard the name Vailima, most likely not even that of Upolu, and Samoa itself may be strange to your ears. To these barbaric seats there came the other day a yellow book with your name on the title, and filled in every page with the exquisite gifts of your art. Let me take and change your own words: J'ai beau admirer les autres de toutes mes forces, c'est avec vous que je me complais à vivre.

ROBERT LOUIS STEVENSON.

Vailima,
    Upolu,
        Samoa.

Monday.—It was, if I remember rightly, five o'clock when we were all signalled to be present at the Ferry Depot of the railroad. An emigrant ship had arrived at New York on the Saturday night, another on the Sunday morning, our own on Sunday afternoon, a fourth early on Monday; and as there is no emigrant train on Sunday, a great part of the passengers from these four ships was concentrated on the train by which I was to travel. There was a Babel of bewildered men, women, and children. The wretched little booking-office, and the baggage-room, which was not much larger, were crowded thick with emigrants, and were heavy and rank with the atmosphere of dripping clothes. Open carts full of bedding stood by the half-hour in the rain. The officials loaded each other with recriminations. A bearded, mildewed little man, whom I take to have been an emigrant agent, was all over the place, his mouth full of brimstone, blustering and interfering. It was plain that the whole system, if system there was, had utterly broken down under the strain of so many passengers.

My own ticket was given me at once, and an oldish man, who preserved his head in the midst of this turmoil, got my baggage registered, and counselled me to stay quietly where I was till he should give me the word to move. I had taken along with me a small valise, a knapsack, which I carried on my shoulders, and in the bag of my railway rug the whole of Bancroft's *History of the United States*, in six fat volumes. It was as much as I could carry with convenience even for short distances, but it ensured me plenty of clothing, and the valise was at that moment, and often after, useful for a stool. I am sure I sat for an hour in the baggage-room, and wretched enough it was; yet, when at last the word was passed to me and I picked up my bundles and got under way, it was only to exchange discomfort for downright misery and danger.

I followed the porters into a long shed reaching downhill from West Street to the river. It was dark, the wind blew clean through it from end to end; and here I found a great block of passengers and baggage, hundreds of one and tons of the other. I feel I shall have a difficulty to make myself believed; and certainly the scene must have been exceptional, for it was too dangerous for daily repetition. It was a tight jam; there was no fair way through the mingled mass of brute and living obstruction. Into the upper skirts of the crowd, porters, infuriated by hurry and overwork, clove their way with shouts. I may say that we stood like sheep, and that the porters charged among us like so many maddened sheep-dogs; and I believe these men were no longer answerable for their acts. It mattered not what they were carrying, they drove straight into the press, and when they could get no farther, blindly discharged their barrowful. With my own hand, for instance, I saved the life of a child as it sat upon its mother's knee, she sitting on a box; and since I heard of no accident, I must suppose that there were many similar interpositions in the course of the evening. It will give some idea of the state of mind to which we were reduced if I tell you that neither the porter nor the mother of the child paid the least attention to my act. It was not till some time after that I understood what I had done myself, for to ward off heavy boxes seemed at the moment a natural incident of human life. Cold, wet, clamour, dead opposition to progress, such as one encounters in an evil dream, had utterly daunted the spirits. We had accepted this purgatory as a child accepts the conditions of the world. For my part, I shivered a little, and my back ached wearily; but I believe I had neither a hope nor a fear, and all the activities of my nature had become tributary to one massive sensation of discomfort.

At length, and after how long an interval I hesitate to guess, the crowd began to move, heavily straining through itself. About the same time some lamps were lighted, and threw a sudden flare over the shed. We were being filtered out into the river boat for Jersey City. You may imagine how slowly this filtering proceeded, through the dense, choking crush, every one overladen with packages or children, and yet under the necessity of fishing out his ticket by the way; but it ended at length for me, and I found myself on deck under a flimsy awning and with a trifle of elbow-room to stretch and breathe in. This was on the starboard; for the bulk of the emigrants stuck hopelessly on the port side, by which we had entered. In vain the seamen shouted to them to move on, and threatened them with shipwreck. These poor people were under a spell of stupor, and did not stir a foot. It rained as heavily as ever, but the wind now came in sudden claps and capfuls, not without danger to a boat so badly ballasted as ours; and we crept over the river in the darkness, trailing one paddle in the water like a wounded duck, and passed ever and again by huge, illuminated steamers running many knots, and heralding their approach by strains of music. The contrast between these pleasure embarkations and our own grim vessel, with her list to port and her freight of wet and silent emigrants, was of that glaring description which we count too obvious for the purposes of art.

The landing at Jersey was done in a stampede. I had

a fixed sense of calamity, and to judge by conduct, the same persuasion was common to us all. A panic selfishness, like that produced by fear, presided over the disorder of our landing. People pushed, and elbowed, and ran, their families following how they could. Children fell, and were picked up to be rewarded by a blow. One child, who had lost her parents, screamed steadily and with increasing shrillness, as though verging towards a fit; an official kept her by him, but no one else seemed so much as to remark her distress; and I am ashamed to say that I ran among the rest. I was so weary that I had twice to make a halt and set down my bundles in the hundred yards or so between the pier and the railway station, so that I was quite wet by the time that I got under cover. There was no waiting-room, no refreshment-room; the cars were locked; and for at least another hour, or so it seemed, we had to camp upon the draughty, gas-lit platform. I sat on my valise, too crushed to observe my neighbours; but as they were all cold, and wet, and weary, and driven stupidly crazy by the mismanagement to which we had been subjected, I believe they can have been no happier than myself. I bought half a dozen oranges from a boy, for oranges and nuts were the only refection to be had. As only two of them had even a pretence of juice, I threw the other four under the cars, and beheld, as in a dream, grown people and children groping on the track after my leavings.

At last we were admitted into the cars, utterly dejected, and far from dry. For my own part, I got out a clothes-brush, and brushed my trousers as hard as I could till I had dried them and warmed my blood into the bargain; but no one else, except my next neighbour to whom I lent the brush, appeared to take the least precaution. As they were, they composed themselves to sleep. I had seen the lights of Philadelphia, and been

twice ordered to change carriages and twice counter-
manded, before I allowed myself to follow their
example.

Tuesday.—When I awoke, it was already day; the
train was standing idle; I was in the last carriage, and,
seeing some others strolling to and fro about the lines,
I opened the door and stepped forth, as from a caravan
by the wayside. We were near no station, nor even, as
far as I could see, within reach of any signal. A green,
open, undulating country stretched away upon all
sides. Locust trees and a single field of Indian corn
gave it a foreign grace and interest; but the contours
of the land were soft and English. It was not quite
England, neither was it quite France; yet like enough
either to seem natural in my eyes. And it was in the
sky, and not upon the earth, that I was surprised to find
a change. Explain it how you may, and for my part I
cannot explain it at all, the sun rises with a different
splendour in America and Europe. There is more
clear gold and scarlet in our old country mornings ;
more purple, brown, and smoky orange in those of the
new. It may be from habit, but to me the coming of
day is less fresh and inspiriting in the latter; it has a
duskier glory, and more nearly resembles sunset; it
seems to fit some subsequential, evening epoch of the
world, as though America were in fact, and not merely
in fancy, farther from the orient of Aurora and the
springs of day. I thought so then, by the railroad side
in Pennsylvania, and I have thought so a dozen times
since in far distant parts of the continent. If it be an
illusion it is one very deeply rooted, and in which my
eyesight is accomplice.

Soon after a train whisked by, announcing and ac-
companying its passage by the swift beating of a sort
of chapel-bell upon the engine; and as it was for this
we had been waiting, we were summoned by the cry

of "All aboard!" and went on again upon our way. The whole line, it appeared, was topsy-turvy; an accident at midnight having thrown all the traffic hours into arrear. We paid for this in the flesh, for we had no meals all that day. Fruit we could buy upon the cars; and now and then we had a few minutes at some station with a meagre show of rolls and sandwiches for sale; but we were so many and so ravenous that, though I tried at every opportunity, the coffee was always exhausted before I could elbow my way to the counter.

Our American sunrise had ushered in a noble summer's day. There was not a cloud; the sunshine was baking; yet in the woody river-valleys among which we wound our way, the atmosphere preserved a sparkling freshness till late in the afternoon. It had an inland sweetness and variety to one newly from the sea; it smelt of woods, rivers, and the delved earth. These, though in so far a country, were airs from home. I stood on the platform by the hour; and as I saw one after another, pleasant villages, carts upon the highway and fishers by the stream, and heard cockcrows and cheery voices in the distance, and beheld the sun, no longer shining blankly on the plains of ocean, but striking among shapely hills and his light dispersed and coloured by a thousand accidents of form and surface, I began to exult with myself upon this rise in life like a man who had come into a rich estate. And when I had asked the name of a river from the brakesman, and heard that it was called the Susquehanna, the beauty of the name seemed to be part and parcel of the beauty of the land. As when Adam with divine fitness named the creatures, so this word Susquehanna was at once accepted by the fancy. That was the name, as no other could be, for that shining river and desirable valley.

None can care for literature in itself who do not take

a special pleasure in the sound of names; and there is no part of the world where nomenclature is so rich, poetical, humorous, and picturesque as the United States of America. All times, races, and languages have brought their contribution. Pekin is in the same State with Euclid, with Bellefontaine, and with Sandusky. Chelsea, with its London associations of red brick, Sloane Square, and the King's Road, is own suburb to stately and primeval Memphis; there they have their seat, translated names of cities, where the Mississippi runs by Tennessee and Arkansas;* and both, while I was crossing the continent, lay, watched by armed men, in the horror and isolation of a plague. Old, red Manhattan lies, like an Indian arrow-head under a steam factory, below Anglified New York. The names of the States and Territories themselves form a chorus of sweet and most romantic vocables: Delaware, Ohio, Indiana, Florida, Dakota, Iowa, Wyoming, Minnesota, and the Carolinas; there are few poems with a nobler music for the ear: a songful, tuneful land; and if the new Homer shall arise from the Western continent, his verse will be enriched, his pages sing spontaneously, with the names of states and cities that would strike the fancy in a business circular.

Late in the evening we were landed in a waiting-room at Pittsburg. I had now under my charge a young and sprightly Dutch widow with her children; these I was to watch over providentially for a certain distance farther on the way; but as I found she was furnished with a basket of eatables, I left her in the waiting-room to seek a dinner for myself.

I mention this meal, not only because it was the first of which I had partaken for about thirty hours, but because it was the means of my first introduction to a coloured gentleman. He did me the honour to wait

* Please pronounce Arkansaw, with the accent on the first.

upon me after a fashion, while I was eating; and with every word, look, and gesture marched me farther into the country of surprise. He was indeed strikingly unlike the negroes of Mrs. Beecher Stowe, or the Christy Minstrels of my youth. Imagine a gentleman, certainly somewhat dark, but of a pleasant warm hue, speaking English with a slight and rather odd foreign accent, every inch a man of the world, and armed with manners so patronisingly superior that I am at a loss to name their parallel in England. A butler perhaps rides as high over the unbutlered, but then he sets you right with a reserve and a sort of sighing patience which one is often moved to admire. And again, the abstract butler never stoops to familiarity. But the coloured gentleman will pass you a wink at a time; he is familiar like an upper-form boy to a fag; he unbends to you like Prince Hal with Poins and Falstaff. He makes himself at home and welcome. Indeed, I may say, this waiter behaved himself to me throughout that supper much as, with us, a young, free, and not very self-respecting master might behave to a good-looking chambermaid. I had come prepared to pity the poor negro, to put him at his ease, to prove in a thousand condescensions that I was no sharer in the prejudice of race; but I assure you I put my patronage away for another occasion, and had the grace to be pleased with that result.

Seeing he was a very honest fellow, I consulted him upon a point of etiquette: if one should offer to tip the American waiter? Certainly not, he told me. Never. It would not do. They considered themselves too highly to accept. They would even resent the offer. As for him and me, we had enjoyed a very pleasant conversation; he, in particular, had found much pleasure in my society; I was a stranger; this was exactly one of those rare conjunctures. . . . Without being very clear-seeing, I can still perceive the sun at noonday; and the coloured gentleman deftly pocketed a quarter.

Wednesday.—A little after midnight I convoyed my widow and orphans on board the train; and morning found us far into Ohio. This had early been a favourite home of my imagination; I have played at being in Ohio by the week, and enjoyed some capital sport there with a dummy gun, my person being still unbreeched. My preference was founded on a work which appeared in *Cassell's Family Paper*, and was read aloud to me by my nurse. It narrated the doings of one Custaloga, an Indian brave, who, in the last chapter, very obligingly washed the paint off his face and became Sir Reginald Somebody-or-other; a trick I never forgave him. The idea of a man being an Indian brave, and then giving up that to be a baronet, was one which my mind rejected. It offended verisimilitude, like the pretended anxiety of Robinson Crusoe and others to escape from uninhabited islands.

But Ohio was not at all as I had pictured it. We were now on those great plains which stretch unbroken to the Rocky Mountains. The country was flat like Holland, but far from being dull. All through Ohio, Indiana, Illinois, and Iowa, or for as much as I saw of them from the train and in my waking moments, it was rich and various, and breathed an elegance peculiar to itself. The tall corn pleased the eye; the trees were graceful in themselves, and framed the plain into long, aerial vistas; and the clean, bright, gardened townships spoke of country fare and pleasant summer evenings on the stoop. It was a sort of flat paradise; but, I am afraid, not unfrequented by the devil. That morning dawned with such a freezing chill as I have rarely felt; a chill that was not perhaps so measurable by instrument, as it struck home upon the heart and seemed to travel with the blood. Day came in with a shudder. White mists lay thinly over the surface of the plain, as we see them more often on a lake; and though the sun had soon dispersed and drunk them up, leaving an atmosphere of fever-heat and crystal pureness from horizon to horizon, the mists had still been there, and we knew that this paradise was haunted by killing damps and foul malaria. The fences along the line bore but two descriptions of advertisement; one to recommend tobaccos, and the other to vaunt remedies against the ague. At the point of day, and while we were all in the grasp of that first chill, a native of the State, who had got in at some way-station, pronounced it, with a doctoral air, " a fever and ague morning."

The Dutch widow was a person of some character. She had conceived at first sight a great aversion for the present writer, which she was at no pains to conceal. But, being a woman of a practical spirit, she made no difficulty about accepting my attentions, and encouraged me to buy her children fruits and candies, to carry all her parcels, and even to sleep upon the floor that she might profit by my empty seat. Nay, she was such a rattle by nature, and so powerfully moved to autobiographical talk, that she was forced, for want of a better, to take me into confidence and tell me the story of her life. I heard about her late husband, who seemed to have made his chief impression by taking her out pleasuring on Sundays. I could tell you her prospects, her hopes, the amount of her fortune, the cost of her house-keeping by the week, and a variety of particular matters that are not usually disclosed except to friends. At one station she shook up her children to look at a man on the platform and say if he were not like Mr. Z.; while to me she explained how she had been keeping company with this Mr. Z., how far matters had proceeded, and how it was because of his desistance that she was now travelling to the west.

Then, when I was thus put in possession of the facts, she asked my judgment on that type of manly beauty. I admired it to her heart's content. She was not, I think, remarkably veracious in talk but broidered as fancy prompted, and built castles in the air out of her past; yet she had that sort of candour, to keep me, in spite of all these confidences, steadily aware of her aversion. Her parting words were ingeniously honest. " I am sure," said she, " we all *ought* to be very much obliged to you." I cannot pretend that she put me at my ease; but I had a certain respect for such a genuine dislike. A poor nature would have slipped, in the course of these familiarities, into a sort of worthless toleration for me.

We reached Chicago in the evening. I was turned out of the cars, bundled into an omnibus, and driven off through the streets to the station of a different railroad. Chicago seemed a great and gloomy city. I remember having subscribed, let us say sixpence, towards its restoration at the period of the fire; and now when I beheld street after street of ponderous houses and crowds of comfortable burghers, I thought it would be a graceful act for the corporation to refund that sixpence, or, at the least, to entertain me to a cheerful dinner. But there was no word of restitution. I was that city's benefactor, yet I was received in a third-class waiting-room, and the best dinner I could get was a dish of ham and eggs at my own expense.

I can safely say, I have never been so dog-tired as that night in Chicago. When it was time to start, I descended the platform like a man in a dream. It was a long train, lighted from end to end; and car after car, as I came up with it, was not only filled but overflowing. My valise, my knapsack, my rug, with those six ponderous tomes of Bancroft, weighed me double; I was hot, feverish, painfully athirst; and there was a great darkness over me, an internal darkness, not to be dispelled by gas. When at last I found an empty bench I sank into it like a bundle of rags, the world seemed to swim away into the distance, and my consciousness dwindled within me to a mere pin's head, like a taper on a foggy night.

When I came a little more to myself, I found that there had sat down beside me a very cheerful rosy little German gentleman, somewhat gone in drink, who was talking away to me, nineteen to the dozen, as they say. I did my best to keep up the conversation; for it seemed to me dimly as if something depended upon that. I heard him relate, among many other things, that there were pickpockets on the train, who had already robbed a man of forty dollars and a return ticket; but though I caught the words, I do not think I properly understood the sense until next morning; and I believe I replied at the time that I was very glad to hear it. What else he talked about I have no guess; I remember a gabbling sound of words, his profuse gesticulation, and his smile, which was highly explanatory; but no more. And I suppose I must have shown my confusion very plainly; for, first, I saw him knit his brows at me like one who has conceived a doubt; next, he tried me in German, supposing perhaps that I was unfamiliar with the English tongue; and finally, in despair, he rose and left me. I felt chagrined; but my fatigue was too crushing for delay, and, stretching myself as far as that was possible upon the bench, I was received at once into a dreamless stupor.

The little German gentleman was only going a little way into the suburbs after a *dîner fin*, and was bent on entertainment while the journey lasted. Having failed with me, he pitched next upon another emigrant, who had come through from Canada, and was not one jot less weary than myself. Nay, even in a natural state, as

I found next morning when we scraped acquaintance, he was a heavy, uncommunicative man. After trying him on different topics, it appears that the little German gentleman flounced into a temper, swore an oath or two, and departed from that car in quest of livelier society. Poor little gentleman! I suppose he thought an emigrant should be a rollicking, free-hearted blade, with a flask of foreign brandy and a long, comical story to beguile the moments of digestion.

Thursday.—I suppose there must be a cycle in the fatigue of travelling, for when I awoke next morning, I was entirely renewed in spirits and ate a hearty breakfast of porridge, with sweet milk, and coffee and hot cakes at Burlington, upon the Mississippi. Another long day's ride followed, with but one feature worthy of remark. At a place called Creston, a drunken man got in. He was aggressively friendly, but, according to English notions, not at all unpresentable upon a train. For one stage he eluded the notice of the officials; but just as we were beginning to move out of the next station, Cromwell by name, by came the conductor. There was a word or two of talk; and then the official had the man by the shoulders, twitched him from his seat, marched him through the arc, and sent him flying on to the track. It was done in three motions, as exact as a piece of drill. The train was still moving slowly, although beginning to mend her pace, and the drunkard got his feet without a fall. He carried a red bundle, though not so red as his cheeks; and he shook this menacingly in the air with one hand, while the other stole behind him to the region of the kidneys. It was the first indication that I had come among revolvers, and I observed it with some emotion. The conductor stood on the steps with one hand on his hip, looking back at him; and perhaps this attitude imposed upon the creature, for he turned without further ado, and went off staggering along the track towards Cromwell, followed by a peal of laughter from the cars. They were speaking English all about me, but I knew I was in a foreign land.

Twenty minutes before nine that night we were deposited at the Pacific Transfer Station near Council Bluffs, on the eastern banks of the Missouri river. Here we were to stay the night at a kind of caravanserai, set apart for emigrants. But I gave way to a thirst for luxury, separated myself from my companions, and marched with my effects into the Union Pacific Hotel. A white clerk and a coloured gentleman whom, in my plain European way, I should call the boots, were installed behind a counter like bank tellers. They took my name, assigned me a number, and proceeded to deal with my packages. And here came the tug of war. I wished to give up my packages into safe keeping; but I did not wish to go to bed. And this, it appeared, was impossible in an American hotel.

It was, of course, some inane misunderstanding, and sprang from my unfamiliarity with the language. For although two nations use the same words and read the same books, intercourse is not conducted by the dictionary. The business of life is not carried on by words, but in set phrases, each with a special and almost a slang signification. Some international obscurity prevailed between me and the coloured gentleman at Council Bluffs; so that what I was asking, which seemed very natural to me, appeared to him a monstrous exigency. He refused, and that with the plainness of the West. This American manner of conducting matters of business is, at first, highly unpalatable to the European. When we approach a man in the way of his calling, and for those services by which he earns his bread, we consider him for the time being our hired servant. But in the American opinion, two gentlemen meet and have a friendly talk with a view to exchanging favours if they shall agree to please. I know not which is the more convenient, nor even which is the more truly courteous. The English stiffness unfortunately tends to be continued after the particular transaction is at an end, and thus favours class separations. But on the other hand these equalitarian plainnesses leave an open field for the insolence of Jack-in-office.

I was nettled by the coloured gentleman's refusal, and unbuttoned my wrath under the similitude of ironical submission. I knew nothing, I said, of the ways of American hotels; but I had no desire to give trouble. If there was nothing for it but to get to bed immediately, let him say the word, and though it was not my habit, I should cheerfully obey.

He burst into a shout of laughter. "Ah!" said he, "you do not know about America. They are fine people in America. Oh! you will like them very well. But you mustn't get mad. I know what you want. You come along with me."

And issuing from behind the counter, and taking me by the arm like an old acquaintance, he led me to the bar of the hotel.

"There," said he, pushing me from him by the shoulder, "go and have a drink!"

THE EMIGRANT TRAIN

All this while I had been travelling by mixed trains, where I might meet with Dutch widows and little German gentry fresh from table. I had been but a latent emigrant; now I was to be branded once more, and put apart with my fellows. It was about two in the afternoon of Friday that I found myself in front of the Emigrant House, with more than a hundred others, to be sorted and boxed for the journey. A white-haired official, with a stick under one arm, and a list in the other hand, stood apart in front of us, and called name after name in the tone of a command. At each name you would see a family gather up its brats and bundles and run for the hindmost of the three cars that stood awaiting us, and I soon concluded that this was to be set apart for the women and children. The second or central car, it turned out, was devoted to men travelling alone, and the third to the Chinese. The official was easily moved to anger at the least delay; but the emigrants were both quick at answering their names, and speedy in getting themselves and their effects on board.

The families once housed, we men carried the second car without ceremony by simultaneous assault. I suppose the reader has some notion of an American railroad-car, that long, narrow wooden box, like a flat-roofed Noah's ark, with a stove and a convenience, one at either end, a passage down the middle, and transverse benches upon either hand. Those destined for emigrants on the Union Pacific are only remarkable for their extreme plainness, nothing but wood entering in any part into their constitution, and for the usual inefficacy of the lamps, which often went out and shed but a dying glimmer even while they burned. The benches are too short for anything but a young child. Where there is scarce elbow-room for two to sit, there will not be space enough for one to lie. Hence the company, or rather, as it appears from certain bills about the Transfer Station, the company's servants, have conceived a plan for the better accommodation of travellers. They prevail on every two to chum together. To each of the chums they sell a board and three square cushions stuffed with straw, and covered with thin cotton. The benches can be made to face each other in pairs, for the backs are reversible. On the approach of night the boards are laid from bench to bench, making a couch wide enough for two, and long enough for a man of the middle height; and the chums lie down side by side upon the cushions with the head to the conductor's van and the feet to the engine. When the train is full, of course this plan is impossible, for there must not be more than one to every bench, neither can it be carried out unless the chums agree. It was to bring about this last condition that our white-haired official now bestirred himself. He made a most active master of ceremonies, introducing likely couples, and even guaranteeing the amiability and honesty of each. The greater number of happy couples the better for his pocket, for it was he who sold the raw material of the beds. His price for one board and three straw cushions began with two dollars and a half; but before the train left, and, I am sorry to say long after I had purchased mine, it had fallen to one dollar and a half.

The match-maker had a difficulty with me; perhaps, like some ladies, I showed myself too eager for union at any price; but certainly the first who was picked out to be my bedfellow declined the honour without thanks. He was an old, heavy, slow-spoken man, I think from Yankeeland, looked me all over with great timidity, and then began to excuse himself in broken phrases. He didn't know the young man, he said. The young man might be very honest, but how was he to know that? There was another young man whom he had met already in the train; he guessed *he* was honest, and would prefer to chum with *him* upon the whole. All this without any sort of excuse, as though I had been inanimate or absent. I began to tremble lest every one should refuse my company, and I be left rejected. But the next in turn was a tall, strapping, long-limbed, small-headed, curly-haired Pennsylvania Dutchman, with a soldierly smartness in his manner. To be exact, he had acquired it in the navy. But that was all one; he had at least been trained to desperate resolves, so he accepted the match, and the white-haired swindler pronounced the connubial benediction, and pocketed his fees.

The rest of the afternoon was spent in making up the train. I am afraid to say how many baggage-waggons followed the engine—certainly a score; then came the Chinese, then we, then the families, and the rear was brought up by the conductor in what, if I have it rightly, is called his caboose. The class to which I belonged was of course far the largest, and we ran over, so to speak, to both sides; so that there were some Caucasians among the Chinamen, and some bachelors among the families. But our own car was pure from admixture, save for one little boy of eight or nine, who had the whooping-cough. At last, about six, the long train crawled out of the Transfer Station and across the wide Missouri river to Omaha, westward bound.

It was a troubled uncomfortable evening in the cars. There was thunder in the air, which helped to keep us restless. A man played many airs upon the cornet, and none of them were much attended to, until he came to " Home, sweet Home." It was truly strange to note how the talk ceased at that, and the faces began to lengthen. I have no idea whether musically this air is to be considered good or bad; but it belongs to that class of art which may be best described as a brutal

assault upon the feelings. Pathos must be relieved by
dignity of treatment. If you wallow naked in the
pathetic, like the author of " Home, sweet Home," you
make your hearers weep in an unmanly fashion; and
even while yet they are moved, they despise themselves
and hate the occasion of their weakness. It did not
come to tears that night, for the experiment was interrupted. An elderly, hard-looking man, with a goatee
beard and about as much appearance of sentiment as
you would expect from a retired slaver, turned with a
start and bade the performer stop that " damned
thing." " I've heard about enough of that," he added;
" give us something about the good country we're
going to." A murmur of adhesion ran round the car;
the performer took the instrument from his lips,
laughed and nodded, and then struck into a dancing
measure; and, like a new Timotheus, stilled immediately the emotion he had raised.

The day faded; the lamps were lit; a party of wild
young men, who got off next evening at North Platte,
stood together on the stern platform, singing " The
Sweet By-and-bye " with very tuneful voices; the
chums began to put up their beds; and it seemed as if
the business of the day were at an end. But it was not
so; for, the train stopping at some station, the cars
were instantly thronged with the natives, wives and
fathers, young men and maidens, some of them in little
more than nightgear, some with stable lanterns, and all
offering beds for sale. Their charge began with twenty-
five cents a cushion, but fell, before the train went on
again, to fifteen, with the bed-board gratis, or less than
one-fifth of what I had paid for mine at the Transfer.
This is my contribution to the economy of future
emigrants.

A great personage on an American train is the newsboy. He sells books (such books!), papers, fruit, lolli-

pops and cigars; and on emigrant journeys, soap, towels, tin washing-dishes, tin coffee pitchers, coffee, tea, sugar, and tinned eatables, mostly hash or beans and bacon. Early next morning the newsboy went around the cars, and chumming on a more extended principle became the order of the hour. It requires but a co-partnery of two to manage beds; but washing and eating can be carried on most economically by a syndicate of three. I myself entered a little after sunrise into articles of agreement, and became one of the firm of Pennsylvania, Shakespeare, and Dubuque. Shakespeare was my own nickname on the cars; Pennsylvania that of my bedfellow; and Dubuque, the name of a place in the State of Iowa, that of an amiable young fellow going west to cure an asthma, and retarding his recovery by incessantly chewing or smoking, and sometimes chewing and smoking together. I have never seen tobacco so sillily abused. Shakespeare bought a tin washing-dish, Dubuque a towel, and Pennsylvania a brick of soap. The partners used these instruments, one after another, according to the order of their first awaking; and when the firm had finished there was no want of borrowers. Each filled the tin dish at the water filter opposite the stove, and retired with the whole stock in trade to the platform of the car. There he knelt down, supporting himself by a shoulder against the woodwork, or one elbow crooked about the railing, and made a shift to wash his face and neck and hands, —a cold, an insufficient, and, if the train is moving rapidly, a somewhat dangerous toilet.

On a similar division of expense, the firm of Pennsylvania, Shakespeare, and Dubuque supplied themselves with coffee, sugar, and necessary vessels; and their operations are a type of what went on through all the cars. Before the sun was up the stove would be brightly burning; at the first station the natives would come on board with milk and eggs and coffee cakes; and soon from end to end the car would be filled with little parties breakfasting upon the bed-boards. It was the pleasantest hour of the day.

There were meals to be had, however, by the way-side: a breakfast in the morning, a dinner somewhere between eleven and two, and supper from five to eight or nine at night. We had rarely less than twenty minutes for each; and if we had not spent many another twenty minutes waiting for some express upon a side track among miles of desert, we might have taken an hour to each repast and arrived at San Francisco up to time. For haste is not the foible of an emigrant train. It gets through on sufferance, running the gauntlet among its more considerable brethren; should there be a block, it is unhesitatingly sacrificed; and they cannot, in consequence, predict the length of the passage within a day or so. Civility is the main comfort that you miss. Equality, though conceived very largely in America, does not extend so low down as to an emigrant. Thus in all other trains, a warning cry of "All aboard!" recalls the passengers to take their seats; but as soon as I was alone with emigrants, and from the Transfer all the way to San Francisco, I found this ceremony was pretermitted; the train stole from the station without note of warning, and you had to keep an eye upon it even while you ate. The annoyance is considerable, and the disrespect both wanton and petty.

Many conductors, again, will hold no communication with an emigrant. I asked a conductor one day at what time the train would stop for dinner; as he made no answer I repeated the question, with a like result; a third time I returned to the charge, and then Jack-in-office looked me coolly in the face for several seconds and turned ostentatiously away. I believe he was half-ashamed of his brutality; for when another person made the same inquiry, although he still refused the information, he condescended to answer, and even to justify his reticence in a voice loud enough for me to hear. It was, he said, his principle not to tell people where they were to dine; for one answer led to many other questions, as what o'clock it was? or, how soon should we be there? and he could not afford to be eternally worried.

As you are thus cut off from the superior authorities, a great deal of your comfort depends on the character of the newsboy. He has it in his power indefinitely to better and brighten the emigrant's lot. The newsboy with whom we started from the Transfer was a dark, bullying, contemptuous, insolent scoundrel, who treated us like dogs. Indeed, in his case, matters came nearly to a fight. It happened thus: he was going his rounds through the cars with some commodities for sale, and coming to a party who were at Seven-up or Cassino (our two games), upon a bed-board, slung down a cigar-box in the middle of the cards, knocking one man's hand to the floor. It was the last straw. In a moment the whole party were upon their feet, the cigars were upset, and he was ordered to " get out of that directly, or he would get more than he reckoned for." The fellow grumbled and muttered, but ended by making off, and was less openly insulting in the future. On the other hand, the lad who rode with us in this capacity from Ogden to Sacramento made himself the friend of all, and helped us with information, attention, assistance, and a kind countenance. He told us where and when we should have our meals, and how long the train would stop; kept seats at table for those who were delayed, and watched that we should neither be left behind nor yet unnecessarily hurried. You, who live at home at ease, can hardly realise the greatness of this service, even had it stood alone. When I think of that lad coming and going, train after train, with his bright face and civil words, I see how easily a good man may become the benefactor of his kind. Perhaps he is discontented with himself, perhaps troubled with ambitions; why, if he but knew it, he is a hero of the old Greek stamp; and while he thinks he is only earning a profit of a few cents, and that perhaps exorbitant, he is doing a man's work, and bettering the world.

I must tell here an experience of mine with another newsboy. I tell it because it gives so good an example of that uncivil kindness of the American, which is perhaps their most bewildering character to one newly landed. It was immediately after I had left the emigrant train; and I am told I looked like a man at death's door, so much had this long journey shaken me. I sat at the end of a car, and the catch being broken, and myself feverish and sick, I had to hold the door open with my foot for the sake of air. In this attitude my leg debarred the newsboy from his box of merchandise. I made haste to let him pass when I observed that he was coming; but I was busy with a book, and so once or twice he came upon me unawares. On these occasions he most rudely struck my foot aside; and though I myself apologised, as if to show him the way, he answered me never a word. I chafed furiously, and I fear the next time it would have come to words. But suddenly I felt a touch upon my shoulder, and a large juicy pear was put into my hand. It was the newsboy, who had observed that I was looking ill and so made me this present out of a tender heart. For the rest of the journey I was petted like a sick child; he lent me newspapers, thus depriving himself of his legitimate profit on their sale, and came repeatedly to sit by me and cheer me up.

It had thundered on the Friday night, but the sun rose
on Saturday without a cloud. We were at sea—there
is no other adequate expression—on the plains of
Nebraska. I made my observatory on the top of a fruit-
waggon, and sat by the hour upon that perch to spy
about me, and to spy in vain for something new. It
was a world almost without a feature; an empty sky, an
empty earth; front and back, the line of railway
stretched from horizon to horizon, like a cue across a
billiard-board; on either hand, the green plain ran till
it touched the skirts of heaven. Along the track in-
numerable wild sunflowers, no bigger than a crown-
piece, bloomed in a continuous flower-bed; grazing
beasts were seen upon the prairie at all degrees of distance and diminution; and, now and again we might
perceive a few dots beside the railroad which grew
more and more distinct as we drew nearer till they
turned into wooden cabins, and then dwindled and
dwindled in our wake until they melted into their surroundings, and we were once more alone upon the
billiard-board. The train toiled over this infinity like
a snail; and being the one thing moving, it was wonderful what huge proportions it began to assume in
our regard. It seemed miles in length, and either end
of it within but a step of the horizon. Even my own
body or my own head seemed a great thing in that
emptiness. I note the feeling the more readily as it is
the contrary of what I have read of in the experience of
others. Day and night, above the roar of the train, our
ears were kept busy with the incessant chirp of grass-
hoppers—a noise like the winding up of countless
clocks and watches, which began after a while to seem
proper to that land.

To one hurrying through by steam there was a
certain exhilaration in this spacious vacancy, this great-

ness of the air, this discovery of the whole arch of heaven, this straight, unbroken prison-line of the horizon. Yet one could not but reflect upon the weariness of those who passed by there in old days, at the foot's pace of oxen, painfully urging their teams, and with no landmark but that unattainable evening sun for which they steered, and which daily fled them by an equal stride. They had nothing, it would seem, to overtake; nothing by which to reckon their advance; no sight for repose or for encouragement; but stage after stage, only the dead green waste under foot, and the mocking, fugitive horizon. But the eye, as I have been told, found differences even here; and at the worst the emigrant came, by perseverance, to the end of his toil. It is the settlers, after all, at whom we have a right to marvel. Our consciousness, by which we live, is itself but the creature of variety. Upon what food does it subsist in such a land? What livelihood can repay a human creature for a life spent in this huge sameness? He is cut off from books, from news, from company, from all that can relieve existence but the prosecution of his affairs. A sky full of stars is the most varied spectacle that he can hope. He may walk five miles and see nothing; ten, and it is as though he had not moved; twenty, and still he is in the midst of the same great level, and has approached no nearer to the one object within view, the flat horizon which keeps pace with his advance. We are full at home of the question of agreeable wall-papers, and wise people are of opinion that the temper may be quieted by sedative surroundings. But what is to be said of the Nebraskan settler? His is a wall-paper with a vengeance—one quarter of the universe laid bare in all its gauntness. His eye must embrace at every glance the whole seeming concave of the visible world; it quails before so vast an outlook, it is tortured by distance; yet there is no rest or shelter, till the man runs into his cabin, and can repose his sight upon things near at hand. Hence, I am told, a sickness of the vision peculiar to these empty plains.

Yet perhaps with sunflowers and cicadæ, summer and winter, cattle, wife and family, the settler may create a full and various existence. One person at least I saw upon the plains who seemed in every way superior to her lot. This was a woman who boarded us at a way-station, selling milk. She was largely formed; her features were more than comely; she had that great rarity—a fine complexion which became her; and her eyes were kind, dark, and steady. She sold milk with patriarchal grace. There was not a line in her countenance, not a note in her soft and sleepy voice, but spoke of an entire contentment with her life. It would have been fatuous arrogance to pity such a woman. Yet the place where she lived was to me almost ghastly. Less than a dozen wooden houses, all of a shape and all nearly of a size, stood planted along the railway lines. Each stood apart in its own lot. Each opened direct off the billiard-board, as if it were a billiard-board indeed, and these only models that had been set down upon it ready-made. Her own, into which I looked, was clean but very empty, and showed nothing home-like but the burning fire. This extreme newness, above all in so naked and flat a country, gives a strong impression of artificiality. With none of the litter and discoloration of human life; with the paths unworn, and the houses still sweating from the axe, such a settlement as this seems purely scenic. The mind is loth to accept it for a piece of reality; and it seems incredible that life can go on with so few properties, or the great child, man, find entertainment in so bare a play-room.

And truly it is as yet an incomplete society in some points; or at least it contained, as I passed through, one

person incompletely civilised. At North Platte, where
we supped that evening, one man asked another to pass
the milk-jug. This other was well-dressed and of what
we should call a respectable appearance; a darkish
man, high spoken, eating as though he had some usage
of society; but he turned upon the first speaker with
extraordinary vehemence of tone——

" There's a waiter here! " he cried.

" I only asked you to pass the milk," explained the
first.

Here is the retort verbatim——

" Pass! Hell! I'm not paid for that business; the
waiter's paid for it. You should use civility at table,
and, by God, I'll show you how! "

The other man very wisely made no answer, and the
bully went on with his supper as though nothing had
occurred. It pleases me to think that some day soon he
will meet with one of his own kidney; and that perhaps
both may fall.

To cross such a plain is to grow home-sick for the mountains. I longed for the Black Hills of Wyoming, which I knew we were soon to enter, like an ice-bound whaler for the spring. Alas! and it was a worse country than the other. All Sunday and Monday we travelled through these sad mountains, or over the main ridge of the Rockies, which is a fair match to them for misery of aspect. Hour after hour it was the same unhomely and unkindly world about our onward path; tumbled boulders, cliffs that drearily imitate the shape of monuments and fortifications—how drearily, how tamely, none can tell who has not seen them; not a tree, not a patch of sward, not one shapely or commanding mountain form; sage-brush, eternal sage-brush; over all, the same weariful and gloomy colouring, greys warming into brown, greys darkening towards black; and for sole sign of life, here and there a few fleeing antelopes; here and there, but at incredible intervals, a creek running in a cañon. The plains have a grandeur of their own; but here there is nothing but a contorted smallness. Except for the air, which was light and stimulating, there was not one good circumstance in that God-forsaken land.

I had been suffering in my health a good deal all the way; and at last, whether I was exhausted by my complaint or poisoned in some wayside eating-house, the evening we left Laramie, I fell sick outright. That was a night which I shall not readily forget. The lamps did not go out; each made a faint shining in its own neighbourhood, and the shadows were confounded together in the long, hollow box of the car. The sleepers lay in uneasy attitudes; here two chums alongside, flat upon their backs like dead folk; there a man sprawling on the floor, with his face upon his arm; there another half-seated with his head and shoulders on the bench.

The most passive were continually and roughly shaken
by the movement of the train; others stirred, turned, or
stretched out their arms like children; it was surprising
how many groaned and murmured in their sleep; and
as I passed to and fro, stepping across the prostrate,
and caught now a snore, now a gasp, now a half-formed
word, it gave me a measure of the worthlessness of rest
in that unresting vehicle. Although it was chill, I was
obliged to open my window, for the degradation of the
air soon became intolerable to one who was awake and
using the full supply of life. Outside, in a glimmering
night, I saw the black, amorphous hills shoot by un-
weariedly into our wake. They that long for morning
have never longed for it more earnestly than I.

And yet when day came, it was to shine upon the
same broken and unsightly quarter of the world. Mile
upon mile, and not a tree, a bird, or a river. Only down
the long, sterile cañons, the train shot hooting and
awoke the resting echo. That train was the one piece
of life in all the deadly land; it was the one actor, the
one spectacle fit to be observed in this paralysis of man
and nature. And when I think how the railroad has
been pushed through this unwatered wilderness and
haunt of savage tribes, and now will bear an emigrant
for some twelve pounds from the Atlantic to the Golden
Gates; how at each stage of the construction, roaring,
impromptu cities, full of gold and lust and death,
sprang up and then died away again, and are now but
wayside stations in the desert; how in these uncouth
places pig-tailed Chinese pirates worked side by side
with border ruffians and broken men from Europe,
talking together in a mixed dialect, mostly oaths,
gambling, drinking, quarrelling and murdering like
wolves; how the plumed hereditary lord of all America
heard, in this last fastness, the scream of the " bad
medicine-waggon " charioting his foes; and then when

I go on to remember that all this epical turmoil was conducted by gentlemen in frock-coats, and with a view to nothing more extraordinary than a fortune and a subsequent visit to Paris, it seems to me, I own, as if this railway were the one typical achievement of the age in which we live, as if it brought together into one plot all the ends of the world and all the degrees of social rank, and offered to some great writer the busiest, the most extended, and the most varied subject for an enduring literary work. If it be romance, if it be contrast, if it be heroism that we require, what was Troy town to this? But, alas! it is not these things that are necessary—it is only Homer.

Here also we are grateful to the train, as to some god who conducts us swiftly through these shades and by so many hidden perils. Thirst, hunger, the sleight and ferocity of Indians are all no more feared, so lightly do we skim these horrible lands; as the gull, who wings safely through the hurricane and past the shark. Yet we should not be forgetful of these hardships of the past; and to keep the balance true, since I have complained of the trifling discomforts of my journey, perhaps more than was enough, let me add an original document. It was not written by Homer, but by a boy of eleven, long since dead, and is dated only twenty years ago. I shall punctuate, to make things clearer, but not change the spelling.

"My dear sister Mary,—I am afraid you will go nearly crazy when you read my letter. If Jerry" (the writer's eldest brother) *" has not written to you before now, you will be surprised to heare that we are in California, and that poor Thomas"* (another brother, of fifteen) *" is dead. We started from —— in July, with plenty of provisions and too yoke oxen. We went along very well till we got within six or seven hundred miles of California, when the Indians at-*

tacked us. We found places where they had killed the emigrants. We had one passenger with us, too guns, and one revolver ; so we ran all the lead We had into bullets (and) hung the guns up in the wagon so that we could get at them in a minit. It was about two o'clock in the afternoon ; droave the cattel a little way ; when a prairie chicken alited a little way from the wagon.

" Jerry took out one of the guns to shoot it, and told Tom to drive the oxen. Tom and I drove the oxen, and Jerry and the passenger went on. Then, after a little, I left Tom and caught up with Jerry and the other man. Jerry stopped for Tom to come up ; me and the man went on and sit down by a little stream. In a few minutes, we heard some noise ; then three shots (they all struck poor Tom, I suppose) ; then they gave the war hoop, and as many as twenty of the red skins came down upon us. The three that shot Tom was hid by the side of the road in the bushes.

"I thought that Tom and Jerry were shot ; so I told the other man that Tom and Jerry were dead, and that we had better try to escape, if possible. I had no shoes on ; having a sore foot, I thought I would not put them on. The man and me run down the road, but We was soon stopt by an Indian on a pony. We then turend the other way, and run up the side of the Mountain, and hid behind some cedar trees, and stayed there till dark. The Indians hunted all over after us, and verry close to us, so close that we could here there tomyhawks Jingle. At dark the man and me started on, I stubing my toes against sticks and stones. We traveld on all night ; and next morning, Just as it was getting gray, we saw something in the shape of a man. It layed Down in the grass. We went up to it, and it was Jerry. He thought we ware Indians. You can imagine how glad he was to see me. He thought we was all dead but him, and we thought him and Tom was dead. He had the gun that he took out of the wagon to shoot the prairie Chicken ; all he had was the load that was in it.

"*We traveld on till about eight o'clock, We caught up with one wagon with too men in it. We had traveld with them before one day ; we stopt and they Drove on ; we knew that they was ahead of us, unless they had been killed to. My feet was so sore when we caught up with them that I had to ride ; I could not step. We traveld on for too days, when the men that owned the cattle said they would (could) not drive them another inch. We unyoked the oxen ; we had about seventy pounds of flour ; we took it out and divided it into four packs. Each of the men took about 18 pounds apiece and a blanket. I carried a little bacon, dried meat, and little quilt ; I had in all about twelve pounds. We had one pint of flour a day for our alloyance. Sometimes we made soup of it ; sometimes we (made) pancakes ; and sometimes mixed it up with cold water and eat it that way. We traveld twelve or fourteen days. The time came at last when we should have to reach some place or starve. We saw fresh horse and cattle tracks. The morning come, we scraped all the flour out of the sack, mixed it up, and baked it into bread, and made some soup, and eat everything we had. We traveld on all day without anything to eat, and that evening we Caught up with a sheep train of eight wagons. We traveld with them till we arrived at the settlements ; and know I am safe in California, and got to good home, and going to school.*

"*Jerry is working in ———. It is a good country. You can get from 50 to 60.75 Dollars for cooking. Tell me all about the affairs in the States, and how all the folks get along.*"

And so ends this artless narrative. The little man was at school again, God bless him! while his brother lay scalped upon the deserts.

FELLOW-PASSENGERS

At Ogden we changed cars from the Union Pacific to the Central Pacific line of railroad. The change was doubly welcome; for, first, we had better cars on the new line; and, second, those in which we had been cooped for more than ninety hours had begun to stink abominably. Several yards away, as we returned, let us say from dinner, our nostrils were assailed by rancid air. I have stood on a platform while the whole train was shunting; and as the dwelling-cars drew near, there would come a whiff of pure menagerie, only a little sourer, as from men instead of monkeys. I think we are human only in virtue of open windows. Without fresh air, you only require a bad heart, and a remarkable command of the Queen's English, to become such another as Dean Swift; a kind of leering, human goat, leaping and wagging your scut on mountains of offence. I do my best to keep my head the other way, and look for the human rather than the bestial in this Yahoo-like business of the emigrant train. But one thing I must say, the car of the Chinese was notably the least offensive.

The cars on the Central Pacific were nearly twice as high, and so proportionally airier; they were freshly varnished, which gave us all a sense of cleanliness as though we had bathed; the seats drew out and joined in the centre, so that there was no more need for bed-boards; and there was an upper tier of berths which could be closed by day and opened at night.

I had by this time some opportunity of seeing the people whom I was among. They were in rather marked contrast to the emigrants I had met on board ship while crossing the Atlantic. They were mostly lumpish fellows, silent and noisy, a common combination; somewhat sad, I should say, with an extraordinary poor taste in humour, and little interest in their fellow-creatures beyond that of a cheap and merely external curiosity. If they heard a man's name and business they seemed to think they had the heart of that mystery; but they were as eager to know that much as they were indifferent to the rest. Some of them were on nettles till they learned your name was Dickson and you a journeyman baker; but beyond that, whether you were Catholic or Mormon, dull or clever, fierce or friendly, was all one to them. Others who were not so stupid gossiped a little, and, I am bound to say, unkindly. A favourite witticism was for some lout to raise the alarm of "All aboard!" while the rest of us were dining, thus contributing his mite to the general discomfort. Such a one was always much applauded for his high spirits. When I was ill coming through Wyoming, I was astonished—fresh from the eager humanity on board ship—to meet with little but laughter. One of the young men even amused himself by incommoding me, as was then very easy; and that not from ill-nature, but mere clod-like incapacity to think, for he expected me to join the laughter. I did so, but it was phantom merriment. Later on, a man from Kansas had three violent epileptic fits, and though, of course, there were not wanting some to help him, it was rather superstitious terror than sympathy that his case evoked among his fellow-passengers. " Oh, I hope he's not going to die! " cried a woman; " it would be terrible to have a dead body! " And there was a very general movement to leave the man behind at the next station. This, by good fortune, the conductor negatived.

There was a good deal of story-telling in some quarters; in others, little but silence. In this society, more than any other that ever I was in, it was the narrator alone who seemed to enjoy the narrative. It was rarely that anyone listened for the listening. If he leant an ear to another man's story, it was because he was in immediate want of a hearer for one of his own. Food and the progress of the train were the subjects most generally treated; many joined to discuss these who otherwise would hold their tongues. One small knot had no better occupation than to worm out of me my name; and the more they tried, the more obstinately fixed I grew to baffle them. They assailed me with artful questions and insidious offers of correspondence in the future; but I was perpetually on my guard, and parried their assaults with inward laughter. I am sure Dubuque would have given me ten dollars for the secret. He owed me far more, had he understood life, for thus preserving him a lively interest throughout the journey. I met one of my fellow-passengers months after, driving a street tramway car in San Francisco; and, as the joke was now out of season, told him my name without subterfuge. You never saw a man more chop-fallen. But had my name been Demogorgon, after so prolonged a mystery he had still been disappointed.

There were no emigrants direct from Europe—save one German family and a knot of Cornish miners who kept grimly by themselves, one reading the New Testament all day long through steel spectacles, the rest discussing privately the secrets of their old-world, mysterious race. Lady Hester Stanhope believed she could make something great of the Cornish; for my part, I can make nothing of them at all. A division of races, older and more original than that of Babel, keeps this close, esoteric family apart from neighbouring Englishmen. Not even a Red Indian seems more foreign in my eyes. This is one of the lessons of travel —that some of the strangest races dwell next door to you at home.

The rest were all American born, but they came from almost every quarter of that continent. All the States of the North had sent out a fugitive to cross the plains with me. From Virginia, from Pennsylvania, from New York, from far western Iowa and Kansas, from Maine that borders on the Canadas, and from the Canadas themselves—some one or two were fleeing in quest of a better land and better wages. The talk in the train, like the talk I heard on the steamer, ran upon hard times, short commons, and hope that moves ever westward. I thought of my shipful from Great Britain with a feeling of despair. They had come 3,000 miles, and yet not far enough. Hard times bowed them out of the Clyde, and stood to welcome them at Sandy Hook. Where were they to go? Pennsylvania, Maine, Iowa, Kansas? These were not places for immigration, but for emigration, it appeared; not one of them, but I knew a man who had lifted up his heel and left it for an ungrateful country. And it was still westward that they ran. Hunger, you would have thought, came out of the east like the sun, and the evening was made of edible gold. And, meantime, in the car in front of me, were there not half a hundred emigrants from the opposite quarter? Hungry Europe and hungry China, each pouring from their gates in search of provender, had here come face to face. The two waves had met; east and west had alike failed; the whole round world had been prospected and condemned; there was no El Dorado anywhere; and till one could emigrate to the moon, it seemed as well to stay patiently at home. Nor was there wanting another sign, at once more picturesque and more disheartening; for, as we continued to steam westward toward the land of gold, we were continually passing other emigrant trains upon the journey east; and these were as crowded as our own. Had all these return voyagers made a fortune in the mines? Were they all bound for Paris, and to be in Rome by Easter? It would seem not, for, whenever we met

them, the passengers ran on the platform and cr
us through the windows, in a kind of wailing ch
to " Come back." On the plains of Nebraska, in the
mountains of Wyoming, it was still the same cry, and
dismal to my heart, " Come back! " That was what
we heard by the way " about the good country we were
going to." And at that very hour the Sand-lot of San
Francisco was crowded with the unemployed, and the
echo from the other side of Market Street was repeating
the rant of demagogues.

If, in truth, it were only for the sake of wages that
men emigrate, how many thousands would regret the
bargain! But wages, indeed, are only one consideration
out of many; for we are a race of gipsies, and love
change and travel for themselves.

Of all stupid ill-feelings, the sentiment of my fellow-Caucasians towards our companions in the Chinese car was the most stupid and the worst. They seemed never to have looked at them, listened to them, or thought of them, but hated them *a priori*. The Mongols were their enemies in that cruel and treacherous battle-field of money. They could work better and cheaper in half a hundred industries, and hence there was no calumny too idle for the Caucasians to repeat, and even to believe. They declared them hideous vermin, and affected a kind of choking in the throat when they beheld them. Now, as a matter of fact, the young Chinese man is so like a large class of European women, that on raising my head and suddenly catching sight of one at a considerable distance, I have for an instant been deceived by the resemblance. I do not say it is the most attractive class of our women, but for all that many a man's wife is less pleasantly favoured. Again, my emigrants declared that the Chinese were dirty. I cannot say they were clean, for that was impossible upon the journey; but in their efforts after cleanliness they put the rest of us to shame. We all pigged and stewed in one infamy, wet our hands and faces for half a minute daily on the platform, and were unashamed. But the Chinese never lost an opportunity, and you would see them washing their feet—an act not dreamed of among ourselves—and going as far as decency permitted to wash their whole bodies. I may remark by the way that the dirtier people are in their persons the more delicate is their sense of modesty. A clean man strips in a crowded boat-house; but he who is unwashed slinks in and out of bed without uncovering an inch of skin. Lastly, these very foul and malodorous Caucasians entertained the surprising illusion that it was the Chinese waggon, and that alone, which stank. I have said already that it was the exception, and notably the freshest of the three.

These judgments are typical of the feeling in all Western America. The Chinese are considered stupid, because they are imperfectly acquainted with English. They are held to be base because their dexterity and frugality enable them to underbid the lazy, luxurious Caucasian. They are said to be thieves; I am sure they have no monopoly of that. They are called cruel; the Anglo-Saxon and the cheerful Irishman may each reflect before he bears the accusation. I am told, again, that they are of the race of river pirates, and belong to the most despised and dangerous class in the Celestial Empire. But if this be so, what remarkable pirates have we here! and what must be the virtues, the industry, the education, and the intelligence of their superiors at home!

A while ago it was the Irish, now it is the Chinese that must go. Such is the cry. It seems, after all, that no country is bound to submit to immigration any more than to invasion: each is war to the knife, and resistance to either but legitimate defence. Yet we may regret the free tradition of the republic, which loved to depict herself with open arms, welcoming all unfortunates. And certainly, as a man who believes that he loves freedom, I may be excused some bitterness when I find her sacred name misused in the contention. It was but the other day that I heard a vulgar fellow in the Sand-lot, the popular tribune of San Francisco, roaring for arms and butchery. "At the call of Abreham Lincoln," said the orator, " ye rose in the name of freedom to set free the negroes; can ye not rise and liberate yourselves from a few dhirty Mongolians?"

For my own part, I could not look but with wonder and respect on the Chinese. Their forefathers watched the stars before mine had begun to keep pigs. Gunpowder and printing, which the other day we imitated, and a school of manners which we never had the delicacy so much as to desire to imitate, were theirs in a long-past antiquity. They walk the earth with us, but it seems they must be of different clay. They hear the clock strike the same hour, yet surely of a different epoch. They travel by steam conveyance, yet with such a baggage of old Asiatic thoughts and superstitions as might check the locomotive in its course. Whatever is thought within the circuit of the Great Wall; what the wry-eyed, spectacled schoolmaster teaches in the hamlets round Pekin; religions so old that our language looks a halfling boy alongside; philosophy so wise that our best philosophers find things therein to wonder at; all this travelled alongside of me for thousands of miles over plain and mountain. Heaven knows if we had one common thought or fancy all that way, or whether our eyes, which yet were formed upon the same design, beheld the same world out of the railway windows. And when either of us turned his thoughts to home and childhood, what a strange dissimilarity must there not have been in these pictures of the mind —when I beheld that old, grey, castled city, high throned above the firth, with the flag of Britain flying, and the red-coat sentry pacing over all; and the man in the next car to me would conjure up some junks and a pagoda and a fort of porcelain, and call it, with the same affection, home.

Another race shared among my fellow-passengers in the disfavour of the Chinese; and that, it is hardly necessary to say, was the noble red man of old story— he over whose own hereditary continent we had been steaming all these days. I saw no wild or independent Indian; indeed, I hear that such avoid the neighbourhood of the train; but now and again at way-stations, a husband and wife and a few children, disgracefully dressed out with the sweepings of civilisation, came forth and stared upon the emigrants. The silent stoicism of their conduct, and the pathetic degradation of their appearance, would have touched any thinking creature, but my fellow-passengers danced and jested round them with a truly Cockney baseness. I was ashamed for the thing we call civilisation. We should carry upon our consciences so much, at least, of our forefathers' misconduct as we continue to profit by ourselves.

If oppression drives a wise man mad, what should be raging in the hearts of these poor tribes, who have been driven back and back, step after step, their promised reservations torn from them one after another as the States extended westward, until at length they are shut up into these hideous mountain deserts of the centre— and even there find themselves invaded, insulted, and hunted out by ruffianly diggers? The eviction of the Cherokees (to name but an instance), the extortion of Indian agents, the outrages of the wicked, the ill-faith of all, nay, down to the ridicule of such poor beings as were here with me upon the train, make up a chapter of injustice and indignity such as a man must be in some ways base if his heart will suffer him to pardon or forget. These old, well-founded, historical hatreds have a savour of nobility for the independent. That the Jew should not love the Christian, nor the Irishman love the English, nor the Indian brave tolerate the thought of the American, is not disgraceful to the nature of man; rather, indeed, honourable, since it depends on wrongs ancient like the race, and not personal to him who cherishes the indignation.

A little corner of Utah is soon traversed, and leaves no particular impressions on the mind. By an early hour on Wednesday morning we stopped to breakfast at Toano, a little station on a bleak, high-lying plateau in Nevada. The man who kept the station eating-house was a Scot, and learning that I was the same, he grew very friendly, and gave me some advice on the country I was now entering. " You see," said he, " I tell you this, because I come from your country." Hail, brither Scots!

His most important hint was on the moneys of this part of the world. There is something in the simplicity of a decimal coinage which is revolting to the human mind; thus the French, in small affairs, reckon strictly by half-pence; and you have to solve, by a spasm of mental arithmetic, such posers as thirty-two, forty-five, or even a hundred halfpence. In the Pacific States they have made a bolder push for complexity, and settle their affairs by a coin that no longer exists—the *bit*, or old Mexican real. The supposed value of the bit is twelve and a half cents, eight to the dollar. When it comes to two bits, the quarter-dollar stands for the required amount. But how about an odd bit? The nearest coin to it is a dime, which is short by a fifth. That, then, is called a *short bit*. If you have one, you lay it triumphantly down, and save two and a half cents. But if you have not, and lay down a quarter, the bar-keeper or shopman calmly tenders you a dime by way of change; and thus you have paid what is called a *long bit*, and lost two and a half cents, or even, by comparison with a short bit, five cents. In country places all over the Pacific coast, nothing lower than a bit is ever asked or taken, which vastly increases the cost of life; as even for a glass of beer you must pay fivepence or seven-pence-halfpenny, as the case may be. You would say that this system of mutual robbery was as broad as it was long; but I have discovered a plan to make it broader, with which I here endow the public. It is brief and simple—radiantly simple. There is one place where five cents are recognised, and that is the post-office. A quarter is only worth two bits, a short and a long. Whenever you have a quarter, go to the post-office and buy five cents' worth of postage-stamps; you will receive in change two dimes, that is, two short bits. The purchasing power of your money is undiminished. You can go and have your two glasses of beer all the same; and you have made yourself a present of five cents' worth of postage-stamps into the bargain. Benjamin Franklin would have patted me on the head for this discovery.

From Toano we travelled all day through deserts of alkali and sand, horrible to man, and bare sage-brush country that seemed little kindlier, and came by supper-time to Elko. As we were standing, after our manner, outside the station, I saw two men whip suddenly from underneath the cars, and take to their heels across country. They were tramps, it appeared, who had been riding on the beams since eleven of the night before; and several of my fellow-passengers had already seen and conversed with them while we broke our fast at Toano. These land stowaways play a great part over here in America, and I should have liked dearly to become acquainted with them.

At Elko an odd circumstance befell me. I was coming out from supper, when I was stopped by a small, stout, ruddy man, followed by two others taller and ruddier than himself.

" Ex-cuse me, sir," he said, " but do you happen to be going on? "

I said I was, whereupon he said he hoped to persuade me to desist from that intention. He had a situation to offer me, and if we could come to terms, why, good and well. " You see," he continued, " I'm running a theatre here, and we're a little short in the orchestra. You're a musician, I guess?"

I assured him that, beyond a rudimentary acquaintance with "Auld Lang Syne" and " The Wearing of the Green," I had no pretension whatever to that style. He seemed much put out of countenance; and one of his taller companions asked him, on the nail, for five dollars.

" You see, sir," added the latter to me, " he bet you were a musician; I bet you weren't. No offence, I hope?"

" None whatever," I said, and the two withdrew to the bar, where I presume the debt was liquidated.

This little adventure woke bright hopes in my fellow-travellers, who thought they had now come to a country where situations went a-begging. But I am not so sure that the offer was in good faith. Indeed, I am more than half persuaded it was but a feeler to decide the bet.

Of all the next day I will tell you nothing, for the best of all reasons, that I remember no more than that we continued through desolate and desert scenes, fiery hot and deadly weary. But some time after I had fallen asleep that night, I was awakened by one of my companions. It was in vain that I resisted. A fire of enthusiasm and whisky burned in his eyes; and he declared we were in a new country, and I must come forth upon the platform and see with my own eyes. The train was then, in its patient way, standing halted in a by-track. It was a clear, moonlit night; but the valley was too narrow to admit the moonshine direct, and only a diffused glimmer whitened the tall rocks and relieved the blackness of the pines. A hoarse clamour filled the air; it was the continuous plunge of a cascade somewhere near at hand among the mountains. The air struck chill, but tasted good and vigorous in the nostrils—a fine, dry, old mountain atmosphere. I was dead sleepy, but I returned to roost with a grateful mountain feeling at my heart.

When I awoke next morning, I was puzzled for a while to know if it were day or night, for the illumination was unusual. I sat up at last, and found we were grading slowly downward through a long snowshed; and suddenly we shot into an open; and before we were swallowed into the next length of wooden tunnel, I had one glimpse of a huge pine-forested ravine upon my left, a foaming river, and a sky already coloured with the fires of dawn. I am usually very calm over the displays of nature; but you will scarce believe how my heart leaped at this. It was like meeting one's wife. I had come home again—home from unsightly deserts to the green and habitable corners of the earth. Every spire of pine along the hill-top, every trouty pool along that mountain river, was more dear to me than a blood relation. Few people have praised God more happily than I did. And thenceforward, down by Blue Cañon, Alta, Dutch Flat, and all the old mining camps, through a sea of mountain forests, dropping thousands of feet toward the far sea-level as we went, not I only, but all the passengers on board, threw off their sense of dirt and heat and weariness, and bawled like schoolboys, and thronged with shining eyes upon the platform and became new creatures within and without. The sun no longer oppressed us with heat, it only shone laughingly along the mountain-side, until we were fain to laugh ourselves for glee. At every turn we could see farther into the land and our own happy futures. At every town the cocks were tossing their clear notes into the golden air, and crowing for the new day and the new country. For this was indeed our destination; this was "the good country" we had been going to so long.

By afternoon we were at Sacramento, the city of gardens in a plain of corn; and the next day before the dawn we were lying-to upon the Oakland side of San Francisco Bay. The day was breaking as we crossed the ferry; the fog was rising over the citied hills of San Francisco; the bay was perfect—not a ripple, scarce a stain, upon its blue expanse; everything was waiting, breathless, for the sun. A spot of cloudy gold lit first upon the head of Tamalpais, and then widened downward on its shapely shoulder ; the air seemed to awaken, and began to sparkle; and suddenly

"The tall hills Titan discovered,"

and the city of San Francisco, and the bay of gold and corn, were lit from end to end with summer daylight.

THE HOGARTH PRESS

A New Life For A Great Name

This is a paperback list for today's readers – but it holds to a tradition of adventurous and original publishing set by Leonard and Virginia Woolf when they founded The Hogarth Press in 1917 and started their first paperback series in 1924.

Now, after many years of partnership, Chatto & Windus · The Hogarth Press are proud to launch this new series. Our choice of books will not echo that of the Woolfs in every way – times have changed – but our aims will be the same. Some sections of the list will be light-hearted, some serious: all will be rigorously chosen, excellently produced and energetically published, in the best Hogarth Press tradition. We hope that the new Hogarth Press paperback list will be as prized – and as avidly collected – as its illustrious forebear.

Some of our forthcoming titles follow. If you would like more information about Hogarth Press books, write to us for a catalogue:

40 William IV Street, London WC2N 4DF

Please send a large stamped addressed envelope

HOGARTH FICTION

The Revolution in Tanner's Lane by Mark Rutherford,
New Introduction by Claire Tomalin

Chance by Joseph Conrad,
New Introduction by Jane Miller

The Whirlpool by George Gissing,
New Introduction by Gillian Tindall

Mr Weston's Good Wine by T. F. Powys,
New Introduction by Ronald Blythe

HOGARTH HUMOUR

Mrs Ames by E. F. Benson,
New Introduction by Stephen Pile

Paying Guests by E. F. Benson,
New Introduction by Stephen Pile

The Amazing Test Match Crime by Adrian Alington,
New Introduction by Brian Johnston

HOGARTH CRIME

The Saltmarsh Murders by Gladys Mitchell

The Mysterious Mickey Finn by Elliot Paul

Death By Request by Romilly and Katherine John

The Hand In The Glove by Rex Stout

HOGARTH BIOGRAPHY AND AUTOBIOGRAPHY

The Journal of a Disappointed Man & A Last Diary by
W. N. P. Barbellion,
Original Introduction by H. G. Wells and New Introduction
by Deborah Singmaster

Pack My Bag by Henry Green,
New Introduction by Paul Bailey

Being Geniuses Together by Robert McAlmon and Kay
Boyle,
New Afterword by Kay Boyle

Samuel Johnson by Walter Jackson Bate

Flush by Virginia Woolf,
New Introduction by Trekkie Ritchie

HOGARTH TRAVEL

The Spanish Temper by V. S. Pritchett,
New Introduction by the Author

The Amateur Emigrant by Robert Louis Stevenson,
New Introduction by Jonathan Raban

HOGARTH LITERARY CRITICISM

The Common Reader, First Series by Virginia Woolf,
edited and introduced by Andrew McNeillie

The Common Reader, Second Series by Virginia Woolf,
edited and introduced by Andrew McNeillie

The English Novel from Dickens to Lawrence
by Raymond Williams

The Common Pursuit by F. R. Leavis

Seven Types of Ambiguity by William Empson

HOGARTH BELLES-LETTRES

Ivor Gurney: War Letters,
a selection edited by
R. K. R. Thornton

By Way of Sainte Beuve by Marcel Proust,
translated by Sylvia Townsend Warner,
New Introduction by Terence Kilmartin

HOGARTH POETRY

Collected Poems, C. P. Cavafy,
translated by Edmund Keeley and Philip Sherrard, edited by
George Savidis

Collected Poems, William Empson